Praise for Belle de Jour

'Belle writes with panache . . . There are some sharp, funny moments' *Sunday Times*

'Belle's writing is fluid and funny' *Glamour Magazine*

'Her writing [is] full of refreshing comedy and eye-watering advice . . . Belle's candid humour is compulsive' *Independent*

'Belle is a natural-born blogger, her style is witty and compact, with the right mixture of intimacy and disassociation . . . Her entertainment value is huge' *The Times*

'Belle's first foray into fiction still finds the former call girl on sparkling and outrageous form, as the escapades become even more risky' *Daily Mirror*

'She's actually really great: fantastically frank, entertaining and clever. I couldn't put this down' *Daily Mail*

Belle de Jour is the nom de plume of a former London call girl. To keep up with Belle, follow her on Twitter at http://twitter.com/belledejour_uk.

By Belle de Jour

The Intimate Adventures of a London Call Girl

The Further Adventures of a London Call Girl

Playing the Game

Belle de Jour's Guide to Men

Belle's Best Bits

BELLE DE JOUR'S GUIDE TO MEN

Belle de Jour

WEIDENFELD & NICOLSON

A W&N PAPERBACK

First published in Great Britain in 2009
by Orion
This paperback edition published in 2010
by W&N,
an imprint of Orion Books Ltd,
Carmelite House, 50 Victoria Embankment,
London EC4Y 0DZ

An Hachette UK company

5 7 9 10 8 6 4

Copyright © Belle de Jour 2009

A CIP catalogue record for this book
is available from the British Library.

ISBN 978-0-7538-2747-5

Printed and bound in Great Britain by
Clays Ltd, St Ives plc

The Orion Publishing Group's policy is to use papers that are
natural, renewable and recyclable products and made from wood
grown in sustainable forests. The logging and manufacturing
processes are expected to conform to the environmental
regulations of the country of origin.

www.orionbooks.co.uk

To Patrick Walsh, Michael Burton, and Genevieve Pegg
— The A Team.

Contents

Preface and Introduction

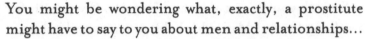

You might be wondering what, exactly, a prostitute might have to say to you about men and relationships…

Let's put it this way: I have met men. Loads of men. Men of every conceivable shape, size and type. In my work as a call girl, I have seen them at their most cocksure and at their most vulnerable. And if this experience has taught me anything at all, it is that this odd and inscrutable species we call Man is often libellously misrepresented in the female press.

The common-or-garden Man is truly a fascinating creature. Whether observed in groups in the wild or singly in captivity, their actions can provide no end of amusement and delight to the educated and discerning female observer.

This is a book for all women who could learn a thing or two about the male species — myself included, because goodness knows my track record of success makes Yeovil Town look like UEFA cup contenders. So if you are after what to do (and more importantly, what not to do) in the company of men, illustrated with personal anecdotes, you will find it here. In excruciatingly embarrassing recall.

Never say I didn't give you anything,

Now, keeping in mind my profession, naturally sex is very important to me. But there is so much more to our relationships with men – companionship, respect, and of course the all-important discussion of who brings whom the morning cup of tea in bed. The carnal is but one side of a fascinating *pas de deux* between the sexes, and we know who really should be leading the dance – us women.

So grab your binoculars and join me, if you will, for a walking tour of Man – his habitat, tastes and habits...

Love,

Belle

CHAPTER 1

Attending to your own needs first

— or, A Man is For Life, Not Just For Christmas

B efore diving in to the world of Man, a few items must be considered. First, do you have the available resources to support a Man? While they may appear undemanding, they require a lot of care and attention, particularly at the training stage. Even choosing a Man is an investment of time.

Be certain never to underestimate the amount of space and exercise a Man requires. While you may be happy to — ahem — 'walk the dog' twice a week, a young, healthy Man may demand more physical engagement than you are able to spare. And his energy must go somewhere — you might come home one day to find an unattended Man has made a mess of your slippers all over the kitchen floor, or even broken out and is mounting the neighbourhood bitch. Ideally, he should be provided with alternative entertainments to ensure this never happens — a video games console is a popular choice.

A relationship will not solve your problems...

The lights are turned down low. Everything is just where it should be — gleaming candles on the table, pillows and other soft furnishings scattered about. Music plays softly from the stereo. You're primped and primed. All that's missing is...

A Man?

It's the old rom-com cliché we all know and love. Girl has fulfilling, if slightly lonely life, replete with gorgeous flat, mysteriously undemanding job, hilarious friends and multiple costume change montages. Girl meets Boy. Boy completes her. And they all live happily ever after. Right?

Erm, not exactly. You'll have noticed, for instance, how nearly every story offered for the entertainment of women — from fairy tales to Bollywood to the shiny supplements in the Sunday papers — ends with a romantic clinch, and preferably a wedding. What they fail to describe is what comes after.

Because frankly, figuring out what to do with the man once you've got him is one difficult summabitch. And if the divorce rates are anything to go by, many people would be just as well off not having gone for the wedding registry, frothy gown and I Dos in the first place.

So before even embarking on a manhunt, it is well

worth considering what, exactly, you mean to get out of it. Would a man – or this man in particular – add anything valuable to your life, apart from a live alternative to a vibrator and an increase in dirty socks on your floor? Is a relationship what you actually want, or even need at this point in your life?

Most of what women are taught throughout their entire lives is not to question the hegemony of coupledom. You meet a man, you throw yourself at a man, and you wait for him to choose you, to get down on bended knee/knock you up/suggest a shared mortgage (delete as appropriate). And whether you believe it right now or not, doing so simply isn't always the best or most appropriate route to happiness.

It may be an old saw, but there is much truth to the saying that it is impossible to love someone else until you love yourself. Anything less, I am sorry to say, is co-dependency. Or as my father (being genetically averse to therapy-speak) put it: be the person you want to be with.

If the list of qualities for the sort of person you want to be with goes a little like:

1) works hard
2) plays hard, and
3) enjoys sex,

then be the person who works hard, plays hard, and enjoys sex. Not the person who sits at home draining a bottle of white every night and listening to her cervix cobweb over.

Similarly, if the sort of person you want to be with is

serious-minded and refuses to get involved with someone unless it has long-term potential, then be the person who is serious and refuses to get involved with someone unless it has long-term potential. Unless you are actively seeking Friends With Benefits (FWB) and one-night stands, don't play with those situations and then wonder why you haven't attracted a long-term relationship. It sounds obvious, but maybe it isn't always so obvious: don't play at being all sex bomb unless that is what you really want.

And finally, have a set of standards, whatever your relationship preference is. Don't 'end up' with someone, CHOOSE HIM. Don't wait for someone to pick you over the other three girls he's juggling, MOVE ON. *Engage your self-respect gland already.* Enjoy life, do things you enjoy, and don't do things you don't. It really is that simple.

...And sex shouldn't be causing you any

I for one think we should be having more sex, more enjoyably, with more partners. Preferably continuously. But then I am biased. Not to mention, often called a slag. Thing is, if you want to call me a slag I'll agree. I'm a slag. And I don't see the problem with it. Why this shame about sex? It is what we're built to do. It may not work for everyone, but it works for me.

It was Philip Larkin who said that life is first boredom, then fear.

If you are at some point bored of a weekend (if anything like me, around 3pm Sunday), take a moment to consider the things you're afraid of, and how that affects the sex life you have.

When you don't go up and talk to someone who catches your eye, because of fear of what the reaction would be... when you don't pick up the phone to talk to someone because you don't want to break 'rules' about how many days between meeting someone and saying hello... when you stop yourself having sex with someone simply on the grounds of what other people might think, or because you're afraid of what someone in a hypothetical future might think about your 'number'... why be frightened of attraction, of flirting, of sex?

> *Men*: Every time you don't flirt, don't phone, you pave the road for those who do — and then, no doubt, you whinge later on about why girls don't fall for a 'nice guy' like you.

> *Women*: When you play games, send mixed messages, give with one hand and take with the other, you pave the way for someone to think twice about approaching you or calling.

> *Non-heteronormative individuals*: just fucking CALL someone and do it already.

In short, it's an infinite feedback loop of people not getting what they want because they're too scared to ask for it.

And the status quo is bollocks, you know it is. They don't hand out Olympic medals to people who only went down the ski jump once in their lives. They don't give awards to the ones who turned up in a load of expensive gear but didn't fancy getting it dirty. What, exactly, are you saving yourself for? Love? Love is love regardless of whether you've slept with one person or one thousand. Love (and I'm sure this is just what Paul wrote to the Corinthians) don't give a shit. So it would please me no end if we finally grew up and stopped equating purity with ability to love and be loved. How many – or few – partners you have in the course of your life is, frankly, your own business. I for one am not going to get to the end of my life and think 'If I could do it all over again, I'd sleep with fewer people.' And if I wouldn't, why should anyone else?

If you're reading this and relate to what I'm describing, make this the weekend. Go to a bar. Chat someone up. Get a number, and call it. Or if you have called, see that person. Tell him you think he's sexy, and you know you are, and that's that. Take him to bed and do it right. If you're already in a relationship, take your partner's face in your hands and say 'I am going to fuck you until both of us can't walk, because you're mine, and I'm yours, and that's the way it is.' Because the only thing between us and the yawning abyss is the warm, wet, willing bodies we meet on the way.

You know what they say – an awkward morning beats a boring night.

Know your relationship preference

One thing that is very important before approaching men is to know your own mind. Are you really up for a relationship, or just a bit of physical comfort? Is a one-night stand your true aim, or are you secretly hoping for the Girlfriend Conversion?

In seeking masculine company we must first practise radical honesty with the toughest judge out there: ourselves. I know it can be difficult to admit what you really are after. However there are extreme risks to not doing so, and they end up on Jeremy Kyle every day. Go in with a clear agenda, and you might be disappointed, but you will be prepared. Go in blind, hearts will be broken and paternity tests may be required. And we wouldn't want that, right?

Right?!?

Fuck buddies, flings, and one-offs

Obviously, as I specialise in extremely short-term (i.e. one hour) relationships, a question often asked of me is should I embark on a Friends With Benefits situation, and if so, how best to handle it?

Men, for some reason, don't need to be told what the rules are. Women do. Why? Because regardless of our natural inclinations, we all know it's not what nice girls do.

Now, you don't necessarily have to be a paid up member of the call girl profession to want a piece on the side. Normal girls experience this feeling too. Believe it or not so do archetypal 'good girls', though they tend to keep it on the down low.

Provided you are fully comfortable with your own situation and your sexuality, however, there is no earthly reason why a nice girl shouldn't. But keeping in mind the requirements of your self-respect gland, there are of course issues to consider.

Case 1: You are both single
Congratulations! You are about to embark on what could be a most excellent adventure. Provided, of course, you follow these simple ground rules:

* *The Sex.* Must be good. Otherwise, why bother? This person is not going to raise children with you.
* *The Companionship.* It helps if this is someone you get on with and see around socially. Puts a nice ending on all those group nights out when it looks like you aren't going to pull (or, pull anything decent). You've pulled before you even arrive. What if he's pulled and you haven't? Even better — take them both home!
* *The Gossip.* (No, not the band, the tittle-tattle.) People who see you out together will assume you're a couple. Get your stories straight and nip this in the bud.
* *The Jealousy.* There shouldn't be any. If you suspect this is someone whose dalliances with others you might be even remotely miffed about, move on, it's not going to work.
* *The Talk.* Must be open and frequent. Nothing sucks quite like finding your fuck buddy has secretly fallen for you.
* *The Protection.* Never forget he has carte blanche to fool around, and so do you. Regular does not equal clean.
* *The Foreplay.* Don't play the whole 'I'm drunk, club's

10

shut, didn't pull, I know you're home alone' booty call shtick. Not more than half the time, anyway.

* *The Threesomes.* With luck, there should be plenty. My FWB standby man N is kind enough—even when we're not fucking—to ask women he's with if they would like to sleep with me, too. Say it together—awww!
* *The Others.* If a potential amour asks if you're sleeping with your fuck buddy, don't deny it. Disclosure might send a third party running, but you were going to have to lie to someone like that to keep the peace anyway. You don't have to be explicit — 'Yes, and just this morning I woke to him wanking on my face.' Just be honest.
* *The Goodbyes.* You must behave like adults. And don't ring him three weeks later from Africa and say you'd marry him if he'd have you back. It's a lay, not a life.

Case 2: You are single, he isn't
Here is a representative sample of the sort of situation I mean:

Dear Belle,

Can you give me some advice about shag buddies? The man in question and I have already been friends for some time. We've done it once now and I would like more. Oh, and he has a girlfriend.

Signed,
    A Reader

Ah, civilians. Got to love them. Seriously though, this goes to show:

1) one great reason why people are so fucked up when it comes to sex, and
2) one great reason why hookers exist.

This is a clear situation which you should avoid, avoid, avoid. He already has a girlfriend, for one thing. Which means, unless you are an exceptionally unusual woman who can't commit, or unless you are a whore (and therefore being paid to leave the premises), it is unlikely that any such liaison will fail to spark some sort of desire for a relationship in you.

Reading between the lines in many such letters, I can see what the writer is usually after is not a 'shag buddy' but a Friend-With-Benefits-to-girlfriend conversion. She thinks that by luring the man in with sex, she can ease her way into his heart as well. Which is ignoring one simple truth about men: they are better at separating sex from love.

Realistically we all know once you've gone this far down the path, then it is going to be hard for you to be friends. If what you really want is a relationship, then honesty is your friend. You should put your cards on the table and be fully prepared to walk. But similarly we also both know you're very, very unlikely to do that. And so the cycle of fuckupedness continues.

However, it is possible. And the success of such an undertaking depends *entirely* on your emotional honesty – and your willingness to be the Ingrid Bergman in *Casablanca* of this story.

So, in order to have a successful FWB situation and avoid anyone getting hurt, you have to think like a whore. Put aside any ideas about a relationship — there isn't going to be one. And if you want to remain friends as well, there are a few commandments to always follow, particularly if there is a girlfriend on the scene:

* *The Matter of Conscience.* Granted, he's the attached one, so he's the more morally suspect. But all that makes you is the accomplice. If you can handle that, fair dues. But if you are secretly hoping for a fuck-to-girlfriend touchline conversion, you can't.
* *The Friendship.* Respect the friendship, as above, always. Don't think the sex entitles you to more than you have had from him in the past, but don't cut him off either.
* *The Distance.* Respect his space. Don't think of reasons 'just to ring'. Don't make things difficult for him if the girlfriend's suspicious. Don't cause scenes.
* *The Meetings.* Meet somewhere neutral for both of you. Hotels are good.
* *The Nitty Gritty.* Use barrier methods of protection, duh. This should be, as our American cousins would say, a no-brainer. You already *know* he's sleeping with at least one other person.
* *The Outcome.* Be realistic. As Sir James Goldsmith said, when you marry your mistress you create a vacancy. Remember that, and keep your ambitions in check.
* *The Truth.* You are an unpaid whore. I'm not judging you, incidentally. Simply a statement of fact.
* *The End.* Let go lightly. It is incumbent on the mistress to be the classy one if — no, when — it goes

wrong. I know, few are. That is why it is even more important.

In short all is not fair in love and war, and the more you play against that rule the less you'll like it.

That Guy I'm Seeing, boyfriend material, and potential partners

When it comes to something a bit longer-term — and here I leave that up to your own discretion — the ground becomes exponentially more slippery. One rule applies across the board, though: for goodness sake, make certain you are both single! There is nothing worse than being painted as the scarlet woman who stole some poor girl's man, even if he was on his way out the door anyway.

So, a rule: if he really is about to get a divorce/move out/split up with her, that's fine. Just say: 'Great, I look forward to hearing from you when you've sorted it,' and walk away.

The bottom line is that any man worth keeping is honest from the start. Life is messy, entanglements happen, but someone who keeps one eye out for the next better thing is not someone you want in your life for longer than a week, because baby, he won't be. Be understanding of any situations — we've all been there, no one's to blame — but firm. Respect your boundaries, first and foremost. Protect your own heart above all.

But... what if he finds someone else in the meantime? you ask.

Trust me, no man can resist a woman who has the inner strength to walk away from him and demand a relationship on her own terms. If he is really serious about being single, I assure you, once he is, you will be the first person he calls.

Now, a few things to look for that sort the wheat (potential boyfriend) from the chaff (all others):

* *The Honesty.* Must be there, as discussed. He needn't be compulsively honest — I really didn't need to know that, in fact, those jeans did make me look fat — but Month 6 is not the ideal time to find out about his three children, either. Aim for somewhere in the middle of that.
* *The Friendship.* If you don't like the guy, there's no point falling in love with him. Really no point at all.
* *The Time Together.* Look for warning signals here, and watch the ones you're sending out. Joined at the hip too soon? Expect drama. Disappears for weeks at a time with no contact? Same.
* *The Laughter.* There's a reason women like a GSOH. It's because it makes the down times, emergencies, and stressful days infinitely easier to handle. Someone who can laugh when you start stropping with PMT? A feckin' keeper.
* *The Sex.* Three times daily, or once in a blue moon: it's rare that people are perfectly compatible in sexual taste and desired frequency, but being roughly on the same page — and willing to discuss and come to some happy agreement when not — goes a long, long way.
* *The Future.* Don't sit him down for The Talk, but don't

15

ignore this either. If he happens to drop into conversation that he never wants children when you were hoping for a litter by the age of 30, *believe him*. If he coos over towheaded toddlers when you need a free and clear decade to establish you career, don't ignore that.

* *The Cold Feet.* If at all possible to do so discreetly, try to find out how his other significant relationships ended. Is he a stayer, or a goer?

I know, it all seems so clinical, which is anathema to love — or so we've been told. You should fall organically or it isn't 'real'. Apparently opposites attract or something.

But that's bunkum. When you are compatible with someone, this doesn't mean you are identical, but neither should it mean you have no common ground. And I happen to be in the camp that believes that falling in love is the subconscious recognition of the embodiment of our most cherished ideals in someone else.

When I met my current squeeze, I didn't know explicitly that his experiences and attributes dovetailed with mine in so many ways — I didn't go down the tick list as such. But when I was single I did spend a bit of time thinking about the qualities that I would appreciate in a partner. So when we met and I noticed that something about him felt right when we were together, the more I saw how that was true. He likes to be up early and bring a cup of tea into bed; I like to wake up to a cup of tea and sleep in. He likes carrying heavy things around; I have a lot of heavy things that need to go up the stairs. We both enjoy frequent kinky sex. And so on.

It doesn't make things perfect, but having a good

mix of interests in common as well as things you can teach each other helps relationships progress more smoothly. And when the drama-meter is reading on the low end, that provides a good base from which it is possible to fall in love.

Know your manhunting style

Be certain not to skip this bit, it's important for the rest of the manual!

Are you at your best in a skintight mini, prowling the clubs looking for fresh meat? Or are you more likely to be found making eyes at the cute student over the top of your cat's-eye glasses? Your preferences in approaching men will tell you a lot — not only about the kinds of men you will encounter and expect to attract, but also how best to handle them. So which type are you, and how should you proceed? Let us take a little quiz and find out...

1. *You are generally introduced to men...*
   a. by family, friends, and co-workers
   b. by the internet
   c. introduced? Who waits long enough to be intro-duced?

2. *The best part of a good date is...*
   a. shared ideas and values
   b. easy conversation and laughs
   c. sexual chemistry

3. *Your idea of a perfect date is...*
    a. romance and quality time together
    b. hanging out and being comfortable, whether in or out
    c. one-on-one... note the operative word, 'on'

4. *When it comes to planning dates, you prefer...*
    a. a cast-iron plan, complete with maps, itineraries and GPS
    b. a rough framework, but nothing set in stone
    c. to play it by ear... who knows where you'll end up?

5. *After a first meeting, a man probably has...*
    a. your name
    b. your number
    c. your knickers

6. *When you're seeing someone, your preferred contact level is...*
    a. daily. Gifts and flowers preferred
    b. random and flexible, as and when
    c. minimum one hour's warning, for waxing purposes

7. *Your commitment motto is...*
    a. if you kiss me, you have to marry me
    b. let's start slow and see where this goes
    c. all's fair in love and war

8. *You know it's over when...*

a. the police escort you from the premises
b. the twelve-hour marathon heart-to-heart winds to a close
c. there has been no contact for a week. Next!

SCORING:

Were you mostly As? Congratulations, you're a

Good Girl (GG)

Also known as: the high-maintenance girl. If you ask men straight out, they will say this is their nightmare woman because she has both rules and expectations. But the reality is, someone who knows what she wants and is not prepared to settle for anything less usually manages to strong-arm her chosen man into submission (and a morning suit). Therefore, most likely to find success in a few, well-chosen dating scenarios and eventually marriage.

Advantages: All women like flowers and gifts. The GG, simply by *expecting* that these are her due, manages to attract more of them than any other type. Men realise, either through instruction or instinct, that this is a lady who requires keeping in the manner to which she is accustomed.

Challenges: Most men really cannot be bothered once they find out about your rules (most of which you probably expounded on at the first meeting). In addition, the ones who do make it through that barrier are probably not alpha-male enough for your tastes. Get used to the fact that your type will be few and far between, and it will be smooth sailing once you do identify them.

 Example specimen: Kate Middleton

Did you tick mostly Bs? Well, hello there

Plain Jane (PJ)

Also known as: the girl next door. Contrary to what the name implies, Plain Janes can actually be rather hot — but always in an understated way.

Flies in under the man's radar and generally manages to stay there through a combination of stealth and inertia. Most often finds herself in a series of monogamous relationships, probably lived with at least one boyfriend, and can expect marriage in her 30s.

Advantages: PJs experience the least disruption to their lives as the result of starting dating and relationship patterns, for the most part because they are rarely single. Serial monogamists, this is your natural peer group. There might be the occasional long dark night of the soul wondering whether jumping from one boyfriend to another is strictly a good idea, but it does help keep the loneliness of the modern world at bay.

Challenges: The Plain Jane has been one half of a couple for so long, it can be difficult to remember her name not yoked to someone else's ('Who's Helen? Oh, you mean *David-and-Helen!*'). Is also so addicted to ease and comfort of just going along to get along that will rarely speak up for what she wants in everything from sex to marriage.

 Example specimen: Jennifer Aniston

Inevitably, if you scored mostly Cs, you are a

Scary Bitch (SB)

Also known as Shedloads of Fun. But blatantly, to a man's point of view, not marriage nor even cohabitation material. Which is fine; it probably wasn't even her priority — that man might not go with the (expensive, deep pile) carpets. If she marries it is late and strictly for a practical reason such as sperm donation, cash donation, or a severely younger model expected to toyboy now and caretake later.

Advantages: The kind of sex you want. Not always when you want it, not always with whom you want it, but sex is out there, on tap, and easy to come by. So if a SB has a single thing on her sex to-do list still unticked, it is entirely her own fault. Also, not having to argue with someone about whose turn it is to do the washing up is the very definition of bliss.

Challenges: No one else ever does the washing up, unless you hire a (very understanding) cleaner. In fact, be prepared to pay for loads of things people who prefer long-term situations take for granted... instead of a steady boyfriend, you have an accountant, a virtual PA, a car mechanic, and a GPS. And of course the inevitable stash of sex toys.

 Example specimen: Jodie Marsh

Keep in mind that just because you test as one type now doesn't mean you will still be the same type next week, next month, or next year. By all accounts I was something of a GG up until I finished school, then a bit of a PJ through university. It was only later that I realised my full potential as a SB. However, what with settling down and all, I expect to revert to good old GG at some point in the not-too-distant future, keeping the SB antics strictly for my man and in the bedroom. So it goes.

You might also find it rewarding to play against type from time to time. Tired of men looking past your PJ charms at the SB in the middle of the room? Realise that inside every woman beats the heart of a vamp, even if it's only for an hour. Fed up with being treated like a piece of meat instead of a princess? Think GG, not SB, my friend, and get thee to the nearest Laura Ashley.

Like with all good dressing-up games, whichever way you seem when manhunting is only what's on the outside. Only you know what really goes on in your heart.

Now on to the good stuff...

CHAPTER 2

In Their Native Habitat

— types and distribution

There are certain broad personality characteristics common to all Men. You are probably familiar with psychometric assessments where everyone's personality features can be sorted along such lines as introvert/ extrovert, feeling/thinking, and so on. A rough sieve to be sure, but in similar ways every man can be said to exist as a point plotted somewhere along each of the following three axes: Northern/Southern, Rufty-Tufty/Metro-sexual, and Intellectual/Sporty. Few men can be said to perfectly embody any of these characteristics, instead moving through varying life stages as he progresses from an irritating little blighter to an irritating OAP.

As an example, Jonny Wilkinson might be categorised as a Southern Rufty-Tufty Sporty (recent revelations re: his interest in quantum physics not-withstanding — the question is not whether he has any quaifications, but if it matters?). By comparison Geoffrey Boycott would be a Northern Metrosexual Sporty. Blame it on that silly hat. My current boytoy is a Northern Rufty-Tufty Intellectual. His predecessor, on the other hand, was... um, the same actually. Never let it be said I don't have a type.

Northern Man/Southern Man

Northern Man

Description — Far from being strictly defined by his geographical origin, Northern Man is in fact a state of mind. Northern Men have been spotted in such unlikely places as Taunton and Ipswich, though are always notable for several characteristics, the first of which is their disinclination to conversation. Northern Man, upon the event of his golden wedding anniversary, may be heard to remark something as romantic as 'happy with that, pet'. This will suitably impress any Northern Girl.

See also — Pete Postlethwaite, Alex Zane in his more contemplative moments, and yes, Wayne Rooney.

A Word to the Wise — 'The reason Geordies have a reputation for so many partners,' grumbles my friend R, 'is because they're so bad at sex. They need the practice.' She ought to know; she's from Darlington. I could not possibly be tempted to comment, but I do think there is something to be said about the relative lack of sex shops Oop North. Porn aplenty — yes. All or even any implements designed to aid a lady in achieving her happy place? Thank goodness for t'internet, is all I can say.

Southern Man

Description — Southern Man, by contrast, is in touch with his feelings, chief among which are jobsworthitude, vague disgust at his partner and work colleagues, and impotent (usually transport-related) rage. Where Northern Man may be said not to suffer fools gladly, Southern Man suffers fools loudly and for the appreciation of all assembled. Or in other words, he won't shut the bloody hell up. Ask 'so what are you thinking?' at your own peril.

See also — Jonathan Ross, Noel Fielding in chatty mode, most comedians who appear on panel quiz shows.

A Word to the Wise — While I have oft been dumped by a Northern Man, Southern Man (all two specimens in my dating history) has an entirely novel approach to ending a relationship: the Passive Aggressive Coma. In short, he takes you out for a drink or meal, and talks at you about this or that incident which in his mind reveals a tragic and irreconcilable barrier to further union, until you achieve unconsciousness. He then takes the opportunity to slip out unnoticed, sticking you with the bill.

Rufty-Tufty/Metrosexual

Rufty-Tufty

Description — Enjoys outdoor pursuits such as rock climbing, hill walking, and trying to mount you in any relatively unoccupied field. Possibly not safe to leave unattended around mares on heat. Shops as infrequently as possible (for all items save karabiners and boots) and owns clothing only in shades of brown, brown, or blue. May be a real ales drinker, but suitably numerous specimens are found among the cider fans. Easily domesticated, provided one's idea of an acceptable home includes three mud-covered pushbikes in the kitchen.

See also — Ranulph Fiennes, Ben Fogle, and the incomparable Ray Mears.

A Word to the Wise — There is something pleasingly attractive about a tousled head emerging from a well-worn fleece, no? Particularly when you know said clothing has been to extremes you have only dreamed of visiting, such as Tierra del Fuego. Ah, the places you'll see together... the outback, the Arctic Circle, Wolverhampton... well, it may all seem like a good idea to follow him now, but I must warn you that sharing a two-man tent with someone whose sleeping bag smells worryingly of chicken soup — as I have had the misfortune to experience — sobers you up on the ends-of-the-earth fantasy in short order.

Metrosexual

Description — By nature indoorsy. May own more grooming products than yourself, or indeed, the local Boots would be able to supply. Does not see any problem with boutique facial hair arrangements.

Many metrosexuals are arts graduates, which may lead to a dangerous proliferation of unlistenable jazz in the home. The rest work as estate agents. Interested in sex, though possibly more as an academic exercise than as a procreative strategy. Not easily domesticated in spite of the neat and tidy appearance – will no doubt prefer his own hygienic situation to your abode.

See also – David Beckham, Noel Fielding again of course, most male contestants on *The Apprentice*.

A Word to the Wise – Once upon a time, I dated a man who was a model. Technically. Okay, so he was on some agency's books somewhere, but a heady combination of drink and self-regard meant he hardly did anything you or I would call actual work. No matter; his parents could keep him in the hair products to which he had become accustomed. Let this be a lesson to all the ladies out there who imagine having a man whose cheekbones you could grate cheese on hanging off your arm might be A Good Thing: check first to see whether his hair-care expenditures exceed his predicted income. If so, save yourself the time and worry and run away.

Intellectual/Sporty

Intellectual

Description – Intellectual man prides himself on his achievements, which are invariably of interest to a select circle of individuals numbering exactly one: himself.

Whether of the science and engineering variety or one of the arts and humanities sort, intellectual man will lose no time, and scarcely any breath, before regaling you with all manner of weird and wonderful trivia about things for which you care nothing. What many women fail to realise is that your undivided attention is neither required nor desired. Simply nod and smile.

See also — Jeremy Paxman, that Ben Goldacre fellow, and would you believe it, for all that kicking around of a football, Frank Lampard.

A Word to the Wise — I dated a man who loved Chaucer more than he loved me. I suppose in retrospect one reason for pursuing such a person was the expectation that he would woo me with beautiful language and I would experience raptures heretofore unknown. What girl doesn't imagine being swept off her feet with letters, cards, and whispered sweet nothings in her ear? Unfortunately for me, it was not to be. Much as he admired the written word, the gentleman was far too careful a scholar to chance embarrassing himself in an unguarded moment of passion. Often, he said nothing at all and when he did it was shockingly in-appropriate. In point of fact his usual term of endearment for me was the familiar anatomical term that rhymes with 'hunt'.

Sporty

Description — This category encompasses the sport participant, which overlaps considerably with the Rufty-Tufty species detailed above, but also the sport fan, which is a more general and widespread condition. Sporty Man has three great loves in his life: his team, his car, and his mum. In that order. The best time to catch the attention of a Sporty Man is during a lull in the football season, the rugby season, the Formula 1 season, the cricket season, et al. In other words a window of approximately twelve nanoseconds a year. Together with Intellectual Man, the ideal pub quiz team.

See also – Gazza, Shearer, Keegan, in fact most Toon alumni, and your brother.

A Word to the Wise – You will, and I am not joking, lose out to the sport. Every single time. It matters not whether you are delivering this man's firstborn son, if the FA Cup final is on, get your mum to hold your hand in hospital. My good friend A1 is one example of the Sporty type – and his long-suffering wife sits in silence while he watches the footy. He calls it a 'mixed marriage'. I call it a season in hell.

Notable subtypes

Now that we have covered in broad strokes the ranges of Manly behaviour, let us consider several of the more amusing modern subtypes found in the wild.

The Modern Dandy

Range – London, Brighton, Edinburgh, and rarely anywhere in between.

Plumage – For summer, the Modern Dandy prefers a Raj theme, something along the lines of the look favoured by Charles Dance in *The Jewel in the Crown*. Linen will certainly feature. Silk, especially in the form of a scarf or cravat, may make an appearance. A light jacket, only slightly deconstructed, will undoubtedly be required.

In winter, the Modern Dandy's fancy turns to all things Edwardian: a stiff collar, a waistcoat, and of course many, many yards of velvet. And they are yards, naturally, not metres – Modern Dandy does not acknowledge metric.

Diet – Anything he thinks might make you squeamish. Lambs' tongues are a particular favourite.

Nest – Struggling to carve out its own identity somewhere between the clichés of a bondage dungeon and an Austin-Powers-style honey trap, the Modern Dandy will most likely decorate his home with inexplicable and disturbing *objets*. The studied air of insouciance will be tempered by your suspicion he just bought a job lot of this stuff from a retired dominatrix back in 1998.

As for music, expect something challenging and androgynous from the many-octaved oeuvre of Diamanda Galas.

Hobbies – Tarot. Throwing come-hither stares at possible conquests. Masochism.

Summary Quote – 'Do what thou wilt shall be the whole of the Law' – Aleister Crowley as written in *The Book of The Law*, forcibly dictated to him by a discarnate higher intelligence known only as... ahem... Aiwaz.

Politics — 'Speaking as a Liberal in the de Tocqueville tradition...'

Exemplar — Sebastian Horsley. Sometime artist, frequenter of whores, Savile Row regular and all-round cad and sometime rake. But never, ever a fop. Russell Brand has his moments. So too does — obsessed, me? Never — Noel Fielding.

Best suited to — Scary Bitches. No one else will be able to handle the narcissistic fallout without decades in therapy.

Often mistaken for — An extra from a Dickens adaptation.

The Likely Lad

Range — Typically born in the Shires and has since gravitated into the orbit of London, whether for 'career opportunities' or as a general sense that he simply belongs there. He isn't wrong, incidentally.

Plumage — Low key and functional, but smart, and expensive. And ruthlessly dry-cleaned.

Diet — Whatever he imagines will impress you. When not in the company of others, ready meals and takeaways with the remnants disposed of in the most hygienic manner.

Nest — Clean, Scandinavian, with everything. Just. So. Close examination of the contents of his medicine cabinet will reveal a queue of identical, unopened product packages behind the ones currently in use.

Don't be tempted to imagine that his well-laid-out environment is in need of a woman's touch: many more than you have been here, dear, and not one has managed to leave a discernible trace of her existence yet. You will not be different.

Hobbies — Whatever is new, now, and next. For several weeks this may be you. Then a new business venture. Following hot on the heels of an adventure holiday, preferably to a place where networking is likely to occur. Actual passion is never involved. The Likely Lad has picked up and discarded more ideas in a single month than most men do in a lifetime, and does not see particular problem with this. Will propose within a fortnight of meeting you or not at all.

Quote — 'What's the value-added here?' Might play for irony when he says it, but trust me, it is never meant ironically.

Politics — Whatever is most expedient. New Labour, once. Conservative now.

Exemplar — Hugh Grant in real-life mode, not as any of the charmingly dishevelled characters he has played on film. The main clue is that HG gives his women identical gifts, regardless of their preferences or taste. James Cracknell. David Cameron. Many, though not all, pop stars.

Best suited to — Plain Janes. SBs frighten them; GGs don't even appear in their radar. If you own any cashmere or clothing from Boden all the better. Hunter wellies optional.

Often mistaken for – A Man Behaving Badly. In actual fact, Likely Lads shower more often (or use more Lynx) and are 10+ years younger.

The Culture Collector

Range – Surprisingly widespread, given the restrictions of his tastes and interests. Certainly wherever imported supplies may be shipped in without incurring too much in the way of import taxes at the border. So not Middlesborough, then.

Plumage – Understated. An artful amount of wear and tear for effect. In a word, boring.

Diet – Whatever Hugh Fearnley-Whittingstall is stuffing in a goose's neck this year. Expensive bottles of wine thrown back as if they were cheap plonk. Bottles of high-end spirit he has neither the time nor interest to acquire the taste for (but they look so nice in the bar). A few guilty-pleasure rounds of cheese on toast, or *une tranche de pain grillé avec fromage,* if you please. The occasional ironic Snowball.

Nest – As far as his budget will extend, in the best possible taste. A framed cover of some vinyl rarity may be employed. A full-wall mural of Miles Davis has been recorded by one of my field reporters. Whatever horrifying Dutch-designed wallpaper and light fixture is decreed current. Comfortable sleeping arrangements sacrificed for something that more closely resembles a fakir's bed of nails as designed by a Danish architect.

Hobbies – No point in listing these, as by the time of

publication our friend the Culture Collector will have moved on, causing him to sneer at any list that might be offered 'that is *so* late first decade millennial'.

Quote – See above.

Politics – As the act of voting is significantly less satisfying than being able to drop the right name or opinion into conversation, the Culture Collector always has an opinion but can rarely be exercised to care.

Exemplar – That fellow on *Newsnight Review*, you know, the one with the loathsome trendy specs. Anyone who owns loathsome trendy specs.

Best suited to – Good Girls, as surprising as that sounds: unearthing a rare gem and transforming her a la 'Enry 'Iggins is exactly in the Culture Collector's remit.

Often mistaken for – Someone you might be pleased to engage in conversation with.

The Eternal Youth

Range – When single: As the natural hunting ground of this subspecies is concentrated in north London, he is rarely found far from there. Unfortunately, because he refuses to sell out, man, he can just as rarely afford to live in the more stylish areas. Will try to convince you that living like a student past the age of thirty is either a matter of 'keeping it real' or 'saving up for a house' (um, he isn't). Expect 'going back to mine' to involve the night bus to Kilburn then. Significant populations of Eternal Youths are also located in many major University areas, or more to the point, in inexpensive areas not far from universities yet wedged firmly and fatally between city cool and stockbroker belt, such as Bedminster for Bristol, Luton for London, and North Shields for Newcastle. Will never admit to this, however.

When attached: If you meet an Eternal Youth who says he lives in Putney, then run for the hills, my friend. That is a MARRIED man you're talking with.

Plumage — Distinguishing between the summer and winter coats of these individuals is simply a matter of counting the layers. Only one faux-vintage t-shirt and a light, ironically hued jacket? Summer. Several faux-vintage shirts, an ironically hued jacket, and a duffel coat? Winter.

Diet — Takeaways, dodgy kebabs. In the first three months of the year may be seen buying an organic muesli, whose box will be gathering dust in his otherwise empty cupboards for another twelve months.

Nest — Crowded with boxes full of memorabilia for bands you've never heard of, festivals you've never been to, and films you'll never see. None of which is more recent than 1995 or so.

Hobbies — Skateboarding (taken up aged thirty). DJing (same). Writing (as before).

Quote — 'As a club DJ I rock bangers that create crazy excitement in the party. The original was a hood classic — so big they made me a "special" — a revoiced version dedicated to me. Shit is straight banging. ATL trap music means JA shottas. It's an ugly situation.' — Tim Westwood

Politics — In theory, a hybrid-driving, all-dancing-all-singing recycler. In reality, can only sometimes be bothered to bring his own carrier bags to the shops.

Exemplar — The old guys you see hanging around small music gigs, resting a lager on their belly and trying to chat up seventeen-year-old girls. The character played by Jason Bateman in *Juno*. Most male NQT teachers.

Best suited to — Plain Janes and Good Girls; actually suitable for very few of either (or indeed anyone).

Often mistaken for — Someone's dad. Do not accept a lift home with this man.

The Nerd

Range — The lower levels of university Physics buildings, and R&D departments anywhere, in the garden shed inventing a wind-up jet engine that will produce clean water for Africa. Anywhere that has ever been described as 'boffin central'.

Plumage — Varies, but is largely in need of a wash. And no small amount of repair. Nerd, I am afraid to say, will never discard an item of clothing with the least scrap of fabric still left in it. Holes in his socks? He'll double them at the ankle. Violet dressing gown cast off from an auntie ten years ago? He won't see any particular need to replace it. A well-turned out nerd with ironed jeans and intact underwear is most likely still living with his (doting) mother.

Diet — Pot Noodle, mainly. Whatever is put in front of him.

Nest – Your worst nightmares come true. Should you decide to pursue this type with any sort of view to long-term happiness, it is best to invite him round to yours early on. Then pay someone to torch the squat where he lives. Result: instant live-in boyfriend.

Hobbies – Trainspotting is for losers. The Nerd relaxes after a long day's computer programming by spending his evenings programming *in another language*. In other words, his work is his hobby. This man is living the dream... the dream of a nerd, anyway.

Quote – 'You've never heard of the Millennium Falcon? It's the ship that made the Kessel run in less than 12 parsecs.' – Han Solo, *Star Wars* (Though of course a real nerd will be compelled to point out that a parsec is a measure of distance, not time.)

Politics – ... is what stupid people do to occupy their minds. Fail.

Exemplar – Patrick Moore, especially when he appears to have some dried food down the front of his suit. While there are many nerds, there are not many nerds in the public eye, but I am confident you know a few IRL (that's Nerdish for In Real Life).

Best suited to – A Good Girl, you might think? Ah, no. Opposites attract, people: this man needs a Scary Bitch in order to really blossom.

Often mistaken for – A geek. In fact, geek is a general term for any person with highly specialised knowledge and sufficient levels of enthusiasm, whereas 'nerd' specifically designates a science or maths geek. Stephen

Hawking is a nerd. Stephen Fry is a geek.

The Anachronism

Range — Henley. Rugby. Twickenham. Cowes. Any-where the place name is synonymous with a sport. Or else in the Highlands and Islands somewhere, where some member of his family owns a sizeable portion of Skye.

Plumage — In summer, a striped rugby top and slightly worn-in trousers. In town, the dread shirt-and-blazer combo. Tweed may be unearthed from the far reaches of his wardrobe, as may something suspiciously resembling a Barbour jacket.

Diet — Anything rich and salty, so long as there are lashings of ginger beer to follow.

Nest — Populated mainly with heavy furniture of the sort more often used to set bonfires these days. An open fire may feature, though there is no guarantee he will be lighting anything in it — Anachronism is a fan of sheepskin and the like, and may also be the kind who leaves a window open all winter long for 'the fresh air'. The smell of dog will feature, as will the accidental discovery of a Christmas card from Prince Philip tucked away in a desk somewhere. Consider yourself warned.

Hobbies — The obvious answer is sport, but only a certain type of sport: sailing, rugby, rowing et al. Ranting at the radio is a favoured pastime, as is raised blood pressure over the subject of foreigners. If carefully handled, you can have a lot of guilty fun exploiting this weakness. While it is not unlikely that Anachronism does have a computer tucked away in some mouldering corner of his abode, it is doubtful that he has ever got to grips with the finer points of such modern communiqués as email, being as he is unaccustomed to abbreviations dating post-1945. And it goes without saying that when texting, he is not unfamiliar with 'SMS 6' flashing up on the screen.

Quote – 'When in doubt, brew-up.'

Politics – As if you need ask.

Exemplar – Boris Johnson, Boris Johnson, and not forgetting Alexander Boris de Pfeffel Johnson.

Best suited to – Cryonically preserved ladies from the nineteenth century.

Often mistaken for – A waxwork come eerily to life.

These subtypes can be combined with the previous definitions to make the definitive binomial nomenclature. For example: Russell Brand would be a genus *Southern Metrosexual Sporty*, species *Modern Dandy*; Ralf Little is genus *Northern Metrosexual Sporty*, species *Likely Lad*.

Others can present difficulties in coming up with a definitive nomenclature: Gordon Brown is undoubtedly *Northern* and *Intellectual*, subtype *Nerd*; however he is a pick-em on the *Metrosexual/Sporty* aspect because although he lost an eye playing rugby, he wears makeup on telly. I leave the final decision on that one up to you.

What can we learn from type-spotting in men? Not

only that there are some fragrant and decidedly avoidable specimens out there, but also that there is much potential for enjoyment. Even the most dubious character has his individual charm. Men come in ever so many flavours that you really must collect them all... though perhaps at a distance. And with appropriate protective clothing.

CHAPTER 3

Identifying Suitable Specimens

As with any collection, unless you have unlimited time – and unlimited patience – it is necessary to be selective in your procurement. Therefore a rough set of guidelines is needed, the better to locate the Men, and to discern which are worth your time and which are not.

Where the boys are

If world population statistics are to be believed, there are more men born worldwide than there are women. I suppose they must all be perishing in Pot Noodle famines or tragic indoor climbing accidents, because according to my single friends, such a thing as an available man is thin on the ground (when not thin in the hair). So where is best to find them? Let us begin with the bad news...

Singles events

Cons: Trade descriptions violation. Always advertised as a sensible solution for busy singles. Always advertised with a soft-focus shot of a laughing young couple sat at a table for two. Always populated by women who far outclass the standard of men present. Always dire.

Pros: You're bored anyway. There usually is a free drink included. And it beats staring at the walls/the cat/Simon Cowell.

Best for: Plain Janes and Scary Bitches, though the presence of a single SB will usually mean the competition doesn't get so much as a look in.

At work

Cons: Potential fallout. If it all goes tits-up (in the bad way), odds are you will still have to see each other and make superficial office conversation every day. And you can kiss your professional image goodbye, if that is something you still wanted anyway.

Pros: Good hunting ground. Unless you are a primary school teacher or in a women's prison, chances are you encounter men in your work day (and hey, even prisons have guards, no?).

Best for: Good Girls and Plain Janes.

In pubs and clubs

Cons: The odds are good, but the goods are odd. Men who rely strictly on loud, drunken, crowded situations to meet women probably come supplied with reasons why you don't want to hear, be sober, or be alone with them.

Pros: You know what you're in for. Specifically, it should be easy to tell if you'll be involved with an alcoholic or –

worse still – a dodgy dancer from the off.

Best for: Scary Bitches and Plain Janes after a few drinks.

Somewhere mundane

Cons: Bunny boiler image potential. In spite of what women's magazines seem to suggest, it is not a brilliant idea to strike up a flirty conversation with the cute stranger you see at the launderette every Tuesday. Men washing their pants generally are best left to get on with it. Unless you are Eva Herzigova. Or the heroine of a chick flick.

Pros: Insight. Hey, you already know he washes his pants. That is at least one box ticked...

Best for: GGs, once they work up the nerve to make the approach.

Amongst your exes

Cons: Forewarned is forearmed. You already know his irritating habits. In excruciating detail.

Pros: Forewarned is forearmed. You already know his irritating habits. In excruciating detail.

Best for: No one. Really. Skip this altogether.

On someone else's arm

Cons: Pariah status. Any female friend worth her salt will stop talking to you immediately, regardless of her current relationship status. No matter how it turns out with the fella, prepare to receive fewer Christmas cards next year.

Pros: Insider trading. You've already heard all about his irritating habits. In excruciating detail.

Best for: Scary Bitches, though Plain Janes often manage to do this inadvertently and typically when tiddly.

Online

Cons: Too many to list – see next chapter.

Pros: Networking opportunity. You might at least make the acquaintance of someone who is capable of providing home technical support at a moment's notice.

Best for: GGs who are better at the written word than in person; PJs who can manipulate the flattering qualities of certain digital camera angles effectively.

'Nice Guy' vs. nice guys

If you've experienced disappointment in your romantic life – and who hasn't? – there will inevitably come the point when, tiddly on chardonnay and in the company of friends, you declare you've had it with Bad Boys and Alpha Males, and all you really want is a Nice Guy. Particularly if you're a GG, and especially so if you're a serial monogamist PJ. And that is where your problems take a turn for the worse.

Permit me to both disappoint a large sector of the male audience, and perhaps mystify a few of the women as well.

If someone describes himself as a Nice Guy soon after you meet, do not give this man your number. Do not accept his offer of a date. And if you happen to be on a date with the fellow when it happens, make your excuses, go to the toilet, break the window glass with your bare hands and stop at nothing to get the hell out of there.

I have some news for the Nice Guys out there. When I hear the words 'Nice Guy' uttered by someone I only know slightly, I think back to the old saying that a gentleman is someone who would never dare call himself such.

But surely we all want to be with a nice guy, yes? Exactly. You see, someone advertising himself as a Nice Guy isn't much of a selling point. The hooker equivalent would be a call girl advertising herself as human — a nice touch, yes, but we should take it as read unless advised otherwise. In the great scheme of things, niceness in and of itself isn't a sufficient reason to fall for someone.

Add to which the observation that most people who would willingly call themselves Nice Guys are, in point of fact, jerks.

Oh, I am familiar with the usual protestations. Some self-professed Nice Guys like to complain (publically and often — why, some sad cases have even made writing careers of this) that women are actually only attracted to men who treat them badly and are therefore incapable of recognising a good thing when they meet one. Which is complete and utter bollocks, and of which more later. And the line is an obvious one, repeated so often it has no real meaning to those who say it.

The female equivalent would be the Look, I Am Really Selective girl – LIARS for short. You know, that perpetually single friend of yours who always manages to get herself into a 23-positions-in-a-one-night stand… and tries to damage-control the situation by telling the man she isn't *usually* like that on a first date. Uh-huh. And I'm just taking money for 'therapeutic services'.

Thing is, there are many actual nice guys in this world. My friend A4 is a perfect example. He's attractive, smart, kind, and burdened with a crippling shyness that means he only realises a girl might have been interested in him months after the incident has passed. Which means in practice, he's far too clueless to go around calling himself a 'Nice Guy' to girls he might be interested in, because he sees them as people, not potential marks. On the one hand, you'll never meet a more caring and generous individual. On the other, his inability to press any of his advantages regularly astounds me. But that's just one end of the continuum.

On the other is the canonical Nice Guy, also sometimes known as the Underappreciated Martyr. You will recognise his usual calling cards thus: uses the word 'genuine' on a dating site ('genuine man'? You don't say? Gee, I thought this was the TS/TV site, thank you for clearing that up…); always stays to the end of the night hoping to pick up stray girls; is physically overfamiliar within minutes of meeting.

Nice Guy will offer help – with strings attached.

They may seem like inconsequential strings, but I assure you, he is tabulating what is 'owed' him in his mind. Meet for drinks and he pays? Go to the cinema and he happens to have already bought the tickets? Need a hand moving a few boxes? Look out, before you know it you'll be obliged to go on a number of pseudo-dates on nights you would rather be doing something else, such as scrubbing your bathroom floor. And there will be no polite way out.

In other words, what Nice Guy is hoping to do is wear down your resistance over time in the hope that you will give in someday — most likely shortly after a breakup, or under the influence of alcohol — and bestow on him a Pity Fuck. And that, ladies, is the worst sort of male lecherousness. The man who *pretends* to be your friend but is motivated by nothing more than the desire to get into your knickers. The man who only sees women as objects, not individuals.

An actual nice guy, on the other hand, sees you as a person first. Possibly a person he fancies, but a human nonetheless. Not a blow-up-doll replacement. Not a mark on a bedpost. Not a way to prove something to the ghosts of ex-girlfriends and bullies who belittled him along the way.

Admittedly, distinguishing between Nice Guys and nice guys can be difficult for a novice. Here are a few scenarios in order to help separate the two:

At a party: Let's say you've had a few too many bevvies, your friends have gone and you do not have enough for a taxi.

A nice guy will: offer a lift or some cash if he can, but if you refuse, won't mention it again. He may ask a mutual friend the next day to check up on you and will leave it at that.	*Nice Guy will:* hand you a tenner for the taxi 'only as long as you meet me for drinks next week'. Or he'll share the taxi, saying he lives in the same direction, and try to get out at yours.

At work: You're a single woman in a new job, and are thrown together with a single male colleague on a project.

A nice guy will: be helpful and professional. He might get round to asking for your number at some point in a strictly social setting, but in general, if he fancies you, you'll be the last to know. If he comments on your appearance at all, it is to helpfully advise that there is still a drop of toothpaste on your cheek right before that important meeting.	*Nice Guy will: always* comment on what you are wearing. Especially if some element of it stinks of the walk of shame (you're wearing yesterday's clothes, or keep a change of shoes in your desk). As with the party situation, help on the job will only be given once you agree to some non-work-related outing. He may propose 'talking about this over drinks'.

In early conversations: Once you've established something in common, you have officially entered the getting-to-know-you period of friendship. Rapport with the man begins to build.

| *A nice guy will:* tell you interesting things about himself, or be interested in the more unusual aspects of your personality. | *Nice Guy will:* steer the conversation towards relationships. Either yours (the better to put you in a vulnerable position) or his (the better to elicit sympathy). |

On a date: Hey, we all have to go out sometime, am I right?

| *A nice guy will:* take you home at a reasonable hour, may kiss you when you part, but will never push beyond the speed at which you are willing to go. | *Nice Guy will:* be 'so caught up' in talking to you that he 'accidentally missed the last bus'. Then will angle for an invitation to sleep on your sofa. As if… |

In a relationship: So you're boyfriend and girlfriend. Now the real challenges arise.

| *A nice guy will:* come around to realising his feelings for you slowly. He values you and doesn't want to mess this up. He wants to know more about your tastes and habits, likes | *Nice Guy will:* come on strong, move quickly, and throw blame at you if you get cold feet. He'll jump straight to the L-word, often without knowing much more about |

and dislikes before falling in love. Treats you the same in public as he does in private.

you than surface qualities. Is considerably nicer to you when he knows others are watching.

Giving gifts: Whether a holiday or a birthday, 'tis better to both give and receive. Or so you might believe...

A nice guy will: give you something he has observed you like or need – or he will ask what you want. Will not push for more acknowledge-ment for a gift, nor more in return, than you find acceptable.

Nice Guy will: buy something showy (such as roses delivered at work) whether you like it or not. Demands profuse acknowledgement and a token equal in value to what he spent. Preferably straight-away.

When rejected: Yes, the road to true love never did run smooth. Ah well. Sometimes parting ways is best for all involved.

A nice guy will: keep any hurt feelings to himself, but proba-bly avoid you in future. If other people know what happened and it comes up in conversa-tion, he will change the subject.

Nice Guy will: get a few insults in on the way out the door, 'I always fancied your friend Emma anyway!' Will phone everyone you know after, to ensure his version of events is spread around first.

Interestingly, there are many similarities between Nice Guy and another type of girl. Let us call her A Relationship Solves Everything, or ARSE for short.

This is the sort of woman who, instead of having a breather between relationships to get the measure of what might have gone wrong and why, has a regular boyfriend within nanoseconds of the last one moving out. Instead of addressing her own problems, being paired off is the sole measure of her self-worth. She probably even has bridesmaids' dresses chosen and a ring picked out. She's looking to interview people for a position, not form a real connection. And woe unto any man who disappoints her along the way.

A Nice Guy will only establish a friendship with a woman with the intention of cracking on to her eventually. A strong clue is the fact that they generally befriend women far beyond their pulling power. Now, there is nothing wrong with aiming high as such — but Nice Guy's refusal to consider less desirable women even to be friendship material should be a strong indication to you that something is rotten in the state of Denmark.

And Nice Guy is results-orientated. To his mind there is no point to being nice for its own sake. To the Nice Guy, if he has put in the time, he expects his reward. While there are a few things in life that have a guaranteed input-to-result equation (exercise to improve fitness and eating to gain weight are the most obvious two), matters of the heart rarely work in this way. A fact which Nice Guy is yet to accept. As he has also failed to accept the observation that being a shoulder to cry on specifically with the aim of getting something in return makes someone a jerk. Not a friend.

51

A word about Bad Boys

Now, about the Bad Boy conundrum… in my experience, what quality women are singularly talented at is spotting Nice Guy bull a mile off. Ironically this is one aspect of what makes Bad Boys appealing: they wear their badness on their sleeves; they are bad, they know it, they don't deny it. They all but scream: Try This At Your Own Risk, and hey, some of us like to. Women can be risk-takers too, you know. But Nice Guys are liars putting on an act to impress us. And if you've any sense as a single woman, that old rope won't sell with you. So you go for the Bad Boys for two reasons: because they seem more honest, and because they seem more Alpha.

It is absolutely correct that women are attracted to Alpha Males. And to the untrained eye, a Bad Boy does a reasonable impersonation of an Alpha Male, especially if you think the only criteria for alpha maleness are good hair and pecs. But while those certainly don't hurt, they are not sufficient qualifiers for the job. Where the Bad Boy has made a slight miscalculation is in translating 'women want a man who is strong and independent' into 'women want a kickass motherfucker who fucks shit up and doesn't take shit from anyone'.

In reality, what we are perceiving in a Bad Boy is Alpha Male *potential*. As regards potential, it is useful to keep two things in mind:

1.) Not every man with potential will achieve it, and...

2.) There's a pretty good track record of men who achieve, then leave. 'Trade up', I think they call it.

I'm not saying Bad Boys will break your heart, but be prepared. They certainly have the ability to do so.

If this is the case, then why are proto-Alpha Males considered so attractive? You have only to look at the animal kingdom. We humans evolved from ape-like progenitors who lived communally, sharing care of juveniles, shelter, and food collection responsibilities. We can't escape the legacy of that evolution.

What sets the Alpha Male apart from the lesser males in primate space are two distinct qualities:

1.) Extraordinary altruism, and...

2.) Excellent Tribe Management Skills.

In other words, a man with a job, who is strong when he needs to be but doesn't misuse the ability. And provides for his loved ones, not asking for a 'loan' when his Ducati superbike is in the shop or he needs to send his black leather jacket to the dry cleaner again. Think Alan Sugar with a heart of gold.

You don't have to be a gold-digger to appreciate what an Alpha has to offer. No matter how seriously and hard you work for yourself, there is an undeniable appeal to knowing you have chosen someone who can support you whatever the challenges. Plus, they often have pretty decent wardrobes without having to be dragged through the Six-Month Man Makeover ritual.

Bad Boys appeal because they look like the men who will be that *someday*. They are strong and can potentially provide. They inspire respect and are straight-talking. However, their Tribe Management and Altruism glands are not yet (and perhaps never will be) fully functional. Keep it in mind, girls. Bad Boys drain your finances. Alpha Males don't.

Our ancestors were the ones who were successful at being part of and maintaining a tribe. Men outside that tribe were generally miserable, antisocial fucktards (same as the present day, really). If you want to mate with a creepy outsider, so be it. But future generations will not thank you. And thus the feminine obsession with Bads/Alphas began.

So what is it that divides the Bads-with-Potential from Just-Plain-Bads? Is there a failsafe litmus test?

Babes, if I had that one figured out, you'd be the first to know. But a good place to start is...

'When his lips are moving': knowing when a man is lying and when he isn't

For several years I had the mixed fortune to date someone who stammered whenever he was lying. I say mixed, because in one way it was good – he wasn't aware of this particular verbal tic and I wasn't about to let on – and in one way it was bad – he stammered a *lot*.

However, discerning when and whether a Man is telling the truth is rarely so straightforward. My mother had a saying: you know he is lying when his lips are moving. It may be harsh, but I understood her point. Unfortunately it is also a point that, when taken to its extreme, can leave you bitter and alone.

So if you've flipped forward to this bit hoping for a step-by-step outline of the physical and verbal cues that will let you know, every time, whether what he is saying is something you can trust, I'm afraid to say... I got nothing. Nothing more than you have, in any case: feminine intuition.

Never underestimate the fact that we have a sense men haven't, and it is strong, and it is most often correct. Men make fun because a) it is something they have no perception of and b) they imagine their decisions are based solely on 'logic' (umm, really? Mixed martial arts cage fighting, anyone?). Our decision-making processes have a less codified vocabulary. Where a chap might puzzle something out, we are happy to go with a gut feeling.

As a sex worker, I absolutely relied on this sense. Intuition is what put my hackles up with clients who, on paper, looked perfectly safe in terms of class, hotel, and income. It let me relax my guard around those who might have looked like a dodgy bet to someone else. Incidentally, you probably already know intuition is seriously impaired by taking drugs or drinking — which is why you should never engage in either to excess on early dates. I almost never drank in the course of sex work.

You don't need to be involved with sex work for intuition to be your best friend. While there is no such thing as perfect foreknowledge, there is rather a lot to be said for the role of intuition when it comes to safety and first dates (or one-night stands). That flash of uncertainty in which you feel ill at ease can be the thing that keeps you safe. This is not to say that it works every time, nor that ignoring it necessarily puts you in mortal danger. Simply that staying switched-on can be your secret weapon, and awareness doesn't cost you a thing.

But back to the honesty bit. In my mind it is an over-rated quality. In fact there are certain times when, in my opinion, knowing the truth can do more harm than good.

Let me put my cards on the table here: as an ex-sex worker, I have a general rule of thumb that honesty is not always the best policy. I would never go so far as to claim the work I did saved marriages, but certainly one hears of more than a few men who use prostitutes as an outlet to avoid having affairs or leaving their wives. Whether this is the best course of action in such a circumstance is... well, their own business, really.

But in a more general sense there is something pathological about insistence on total honesty. The exact number of people I have slept with? Honey, even I don't know the answer, so any man who insists on a full and frank reckoning of that area of my life is bound to be disappointed. Likewise, I am singularly uninterested in exactly what that one-night stand of his sounded like when she came, or where in his flat his ex preferred to give him blowjobs. There is the possibility that a mental image will arise that you are never able to shake, and somewhere down the line, at least one party will come to regret total honesty.

Before even broaching the subject of sorting out the lies from the truth, it is useful to have some idea exactly what you expect him to be truthful *about*. For some people sexual disclosure is important; for others, financial concerns come top of the list. My friend L and I agree we would never have been able to live a single minute with each other's ex. Mine was a serial cheater, which I could — just about — forgive (until I couldn't anymore); hers a problem gambler whose debts she could — just about — forgive (until faced with the reality of what marrying this man would have done to her credit history). Horses for courses, as they say. Best to sit down and make an explicit list — your answers will vary, of course, but mine goes a bit like this:

I expect total honesty about:

* Any history of unprotected sex, just the dates will do thank you.
* Similarly with any sexual health diagnoses. I like to think honesty about this falls in to the category of Common Human Decency, but given the STI infection rates, I think we can assume for most people it doesn't.
* The number of exes I can expect to meet, and how involved they still are in his life. I do not plan to dethrone any of them, but forewarned is forearmed.
* Where he is if I ask, in a general sense. GPS coordinates are unnecessary, but if he says he is at John's when he is later found to have been at Jane's, the fur will fly.

* Money. Where it comes from, how it's spent, and most of all, what debts and responsibilities he may be carrying. I don't demand total fusing of all accounts, nor even think that is a good idea. But if the bounty hunters are soon to come knocking, it's best I was prepared.

But please, don't go here:

* Which lover, specifically, was best in bed. I like to think I will shortly have that designation thank you very much.
* Fleeting attractions he does not act on are permissible – I don't mind where a man gets his appetite so long as he eats at home. Enumerating all of them? A distinct no-no.
* The mind-numbing details of his day at work, his hour in the gym, what he thought about in the car on the way home.... I'm a big-picture girl. Just give us the highlights, ta very much.
* Which of my unchangeable attributes you find unattractive or off-putting. It was years before I could forget that comment about the way I chew my food. In fact, I never forgot. That was fifteen years ago.
* The porn collection. Unless of course he plans to share.

Obviously these vary from woman to woman. But it is good to have a road map of your expectations, because later on if a man accuses you of being mysterious or changing the playing field unexpectedly – and he will – you need a defence along the lines of, 'actually, there are only a few things I need you to be honest about, and here they are…'. Having a short list appeals to a man's sense of logic. He will respect the list. Even if the list consists of exactly one point: Every Thing You Do, Ever.

This is not to say the criteria never shift. Even a sexually confident woman may find her boundaries challenged from time to time. Not long ago I started seeing a man and was concerned about the concentration of attractive young females in his line of work (essentially, everyone but him). And the fact that this new job coincided with increased time pressures in his life, so I was starting to feel somewhat neglected. Yes, I was feeling insecure. I voiced my concerns to my female friend M.

Let me just say, when it comes to men, M is a natural. She seems to understand on the cellular level what other women need years of experience to learn, and still may never get. There are always 2–3 quality men chasing her, and she seems to juggle them effortlessly. And because she is so appealing to them, and so natural about it, she has never had the sort of appallingly horrific experience of cheating and protracted breakup that most of us seem to experience putting her off men forever.

In other words, she is what we might colloquially know as a Smug Bitch.

But on the other hand, she is a useful smug bitch to have around, precisely because she seems to understand the male point of view so well, and how best to deal with them.

So I was telling M about the situation with this man. She stopped me, and said this:

'Listen, you have several scenarios here. You can spend the next six months worrying that he's cheating, and if he is, break up. Then you've had six months of pain, and you think he's a jerk forever.

'Or you can spend the six months worrying and find out he isn't cheating, in which case you're the jerk.

'Alternatively, you can not worry about it. Because if he is cheating and then is found out — and they are always found out — you just dump him, dust yourself off, and move on. You will be fine.

'And if he isn't cheating, and you didn't spend the time driving yourself and him crazy, then what you have is a good relationship.'

When she put it that way it was as if a light had gone off above my head (in fact it was just the compact fluorescent bulb in the room finally springing into full illumination). She was right — it didn't matter whether I worried or not, because men are actually terrible liars, and eventually will always be found out. I didn't need to do a thing. Female intuition, whether they acknowledge it or not, will always beat even the most experienced liar. I just had to sit back, enjoy the ride, and let what would eventually happen happen.

As it turned out in the end, we split up, he tried it on with a co-worker, and she rejected him. But because I hadn't spent much time worrying about it, when I found out what had happened, once we were no longer together, it neither bothered me nor shook my self-image. M was right: I was fine.

CHAPTER 4

Dating

— the wheat, the chaff, and the numbers game

Time was when you met men through your place of worship, your meddling relatives, or a dodgy contact ad. No more. There are as many ways to meet men these days, it would seem, as there are men.

From t'internet to real life, fully half of the world's population is male. This is a good thing: they're out there for the taking. But it also has its drawbacks: how to sort through the relentless look-at-me self promotion of matchmaking websites, speed dating and the rest?

Internet dating

Ah, the internet. With it we can order almost everything to be delivered directly to our doors, from the weekly shop to books to, yes, men. Because there are a lot of men out there with spare time, a reasonably decent connection, and most importantly, the airtight conviction that anything is better if they can do it sitting in their front rooms wearing only their pants.

Yes, ladies, it's a buyer's market out there, and we are in charge. In theory.

I've dabbled in internet dating with varying success, but the best email I got was:

'Please contact me, you're just the right height!'

I was too scared to ask what for!

The people who believe that internet dating is only for sad weirdoes with no social skills are wrong. I mean, it's for them too, but it is also increasingly appropriate to hint — though not yet directly confirm — that you met your beloved in the Random Hookups section of the local online adverts.

Internet dating is certainly less laughable now than it was only several years ago. Still, it can be off-putting especially when you look at the media coverage. Stories about couples 'cheating' with someone they know only through Second Life is... well, it's the modern equivalent of marrying men on Death Row — a phenomenon confined almost entirely to overweight trailer inhabitants of the Southern US states, and inadvisable for anyone regardless of where they live.

But if you look on internet dating as a simple tool for meeting people, it isn't terrible. You can (usually) see what someone looks like before deciding to respond. You can (usually) tell a bit about his tastes and whether they mesh with yours. Most importantly, you can (usually) get some idea about his skills as a writer.

That is correct — I judge a man's mating potential largely by his grasp of grammar and spelling. I know, I'm a harsh bitch. But just between us girls, let's be honest: you wouldn't really want to date someone who writes full emails in txt-spk, would you? Or who suffers from an acute case of Greengrocer's Apostrophe's.

However, it is important to remember that what you see is not necessarily what you will get. Do you already have an online profile? Good, then I don't have to describe the hours of cropping, blurring and outright airbrushing that go into the selection of an appropriate photo.

Whoever said you can't judge a book by its cover was wrong. In real life your date might be three feet shorter than he mentioned, or three stone heavier, or indeed that photo might have been taken in 1992. But what people choose to put online as a visual representation of themselves speaks volumes. In fact it is something like choosing a call girl from a website.

What to expect

There are amazing people to be found online, you know. And there are also the creeps. Broadly speaking, there are six types of men on internet dating sites you want to avoid. Or as my lovely editor put it, 'While attraction is quite often unique, repulsion can be common'. Amen to that, sister. So here's a brief guide to the dross:

1. The 'Nice Guy'

What he writes: I'm just a genuine guy into the normal things. I don't know if this is going to work, so I'm giving it one last shot. I guess there isn't anyone

genuine on here, but your profile seemed normal. I
have a lot of genuine, normal hobbies and would
like to get to know someone better. Meet for dinner,
drinks, maybe more…?

What he means: I'm an ugly bastard. If you don't message
me back, that means you're shallow. In fact, you
should go out with me because if you don't, you're a
bitch who judges by appearances. So go on. Prove
that you're not like other girls. Make a bitter man's
day. If you message me back, I'll love you forever. If
you don't, I'll rape your cat.

What he wants: A PJ who will put up with him, flaws and
all. And there are many. Oh so many.

What he'll get: A GG who will secretly despise everything
he says and does but be far too polite to say.

2. The Gold-Digger-Digger

What he writes: I'm very rich and you're obviously a
special lady. So special in fact that this message is just
for you. Of course I haven't cut and pasted it and
sent it to every hot 18–24-year-old in London. No.
You're special. I have a Porsche.

What he means: I'm in my 50s, divorced twice, and have
three children to support. You can meet me in my
one-bed flat, which I will say is just my crash pad in
London – in fact it's all I have. The Porsche is real,
though. In spite of the fact it hasn't been in running
order since 1978.

What he wants: A PJ who looks and fucks like a SB.

What he'll get: A SB who looks and fucks like a PJ.

3. The Conscientious Profile-Reader

What he writes: I see that you like Monty Python. I too like Monty Python. I see that you have an interest in mathematics. I have a GSCE in Maths. I have to admit, I know little about classical music but I do love to listen to Classic FM late at night. We obviously have much in common.

What he means: I have no personality. None! And my only relationship experience is this one girl I dated for three weeks at uni. Okay, three days. Okay, she took me home and then avoided my calls for two days then her brother told me never to contact her again or he would beat me senseless. Please reply.

What he wants: A GG who will take the time to curate all the details of his uniqueness just as he will hers.

What he'll get: A warning from the police the third time he's caught lurking in her garden.

4. The Cyber

What he writes: ur well fit u wana chat? msg me kthxbye

What he means: ur well fit u wana chat? msg me kthxbye

What he wants: Any woman who is well fit, wants 2 chat, and will msg him.

What he'll get: Radio silence from any sensible individuals.

5. The Potential Soulmate

What he writes: I recently read your profile and felt touched by your presence. Two brilliant minds can find solace together as we pass through the vast space alone inside our eyes gazing for eternity in endeavour to turn as we speak above the waters under our feet.

What he means: I would be perfect for you if only it weren't for the irreconcilable conflicts in our star signs. I will drain your bank account and get caught screwing a nineteen-year-old yoga instructor on your floor. Wait, I thought you said you were open minded? Anyway. If you take it badly that's your trip. Peace out, man.

What he wants: A SB who can fund his lifestyle and keep him in the manner to which he will very quickly become accustomed, along with a stream of hot friends for him to cheat with.

What he'll get: A PJ with hippie-ish tendencies.

6. The Sensitive Type

What he writes: I'm a sensitive guy, not like the others. In fact most of the women who know me say I'm a real catch, and so does my mother. I like romantic picnics out, romantic weekends away, and romantic dreams with a romantic girl. I want to make some woman my queen. Are you her?

What he means: I cry when I watch Forrest Gump. I cry when I watch Tom and Jerry. In fact, I cry pretty much constantly since I'm such a sensitive type. When I'm not blubbing over *Celebrity Masterchef*, other hobbies include burning CDs of soppy music and writing poetry. Yes, I really think you're going to go weak-kneed over some buffoon who spends his free time penning execrable poetry. If you don't message me back I'll probably slit my wrists.

What he wants: A good smack about the face and neck.

What he'll get: An unfortunate GG who, with luck, will extricate herself from the horror before getting knocked up.

How to read — and write — a profile

Internet dating has its own language. 'Euphemistic' is one way of putting it. 'Total and uncontrolled bullshit' is another. I prefer to think the truth lies somewhere in between. But it is useful to know about the — shall we say — code men are liable to use online, and how those correspond with the reality you can expect on meeting. Here is what men mean when they write:

* Adventurous = will ask you to shit on his chest during sex
* Uninhibited = nudist
* Sensitive = psychopath
* Wanna chat sometime? = wanna have cybersex sometime?
* ur stunning = I've only looked at your picture
* Looking for a special lady = looking for a pretty but dumb lady
* No fat chix = I really haven't given any thought as to how this might be interpreted by today's women who think anything above a size 8 is 'fat'
* I hate writing about myself = I'm trying to sound charming and modest

* I have a webcam if ur interested = dear God, don't even go there

In the same way that we have certain clues as to whether or not a potential mate is right for us, so do men. So if you happen to be casting about in the small ads or internet for a date, be careful of the language you use, because it could be sending unattractive signals to him. Here are a few choice gems, and what they really say to the men reading them:

* Ambitious = will bore him to tears about her career
* Outgoing = promiscuous
* Spirited = will get into a fight en route to date
* Australian = all of the above
* Likes keeping fit = has been to the gym once in five years
* Kind hearted = recently dumped and on the rebound
* Bit mad = bit boring
* Enjoys a drink = wants him to fund an evening of piss artistry
* Loves animals = desperately wants kids, but has cats instead
* Loves kids = has four, wants someone — anyone — to pick up the tab
* Where have all the nice men gone? = all local men already give her a wide berth
* Enjoys wine = enjoys Lambrini by the bucketload
* Likes to travel = went to Ibiza once
* Loves films = loves chickflicks about someone's new pair of shoes which star Hugh Grant

* Loves books = as above but in paperback
* Caring = potential stalker
* Bubbly = irritating
* Nursing professional = will drink him under the table and tell frightening stories
* Ladylike = carries brick in her handbag

Online photos

You might imagine the forethought and preparation involved would lead everyone to put up the most flattering angle of themselves possible. You imagine wrong. Many people actually do not seem to have any notion of what flatters them, nor care. Phew — you've just saved yourself loads of time. If someone can't be bothered to put his best foot forward in 2D, what are the odds you'll be pleased with the 3D version?

As for the ones who do pass muster, you can still pick up valuable clues from the content of their photos. But there are key differences between the sexes — what looks like a fun, interesting photo when the subject is a woman, would send entirely the wrong message if the subject were male, and vice-versa. Here are a few rules to live by:

If the photo is handheld and from above

Women: Cleavage is the main selling point. You don't even want to ask about the arse.	*Men:* At least you can be confident of any male pattern baldness issues up front.

If the photo is black and white

Women: All the better to hide the Photoshopping with.	*Men:* Is not yet capable of switching his phone camera into 'colour' mode.

If the photo shows a group of friends

Women: Look! I'm popular! If you buy me drinks, there might be a threesome too!	*Men:* A minimum of one of the women in the photo will be his ex.

If the photo clearly crops out a group of friends

Women: My friends are pretty, and you won't meet them. For a long time.	*Men:* Is still married.

From 2D to 3D: meeting In Real Life

Having identified someone whose photo is not repulsive, and whose grasp of the English language is acceptable, and whose communications do not have you reaching to ring 999, the next step is getting to know more over email. Or so you would think. Unfortunately too many people fall into the trap I like to call the Cyrano de Bergerac.

Exchanging flirty emails – and even instant messaging – is fun. But be sure to reserve all judgements until you have *met him in person*. This can not be emphasised enough. Under no circumstances do you want to fall in love with a carefully crafted façade only to learn that in real life the chemistry between you goes

71

nowhere. For one thing, it will be a waste of your time. For another, when you finally do meet and it goes wrong, you will feel obliged out of politeness to see out the date. And he will try to press his verbal advantage. Which takes you into a Nice Guy situation.

So what is the right amount of time between initial contact and meeting someone? My rule of thumb is three contacts. They can be emails, texts, phone calls, whatever: three, as the song memorably put it, is the magic number. Over any length of time. It makes no difference who suggests the date; after a reasonable amount of contact, if he doesn't, you should. If he won't make firm plans — as in, date, time and place — after three contacts, don't meet this person, he's trying to hide something. Maybe he smells of onions. Maybe he has eight children by different women. Maybe his mother insists on chaperoning. It doesn't matter. Don't meet this man.

Holding to the Rule of Three has other advantages: one of the points of internet dating is to be introduced to loads of potential dates, quickly. Spending too much time on any one may mean you miss an eligible other. Now, I realise in this country the dating around idea has been slow to take hold. We generally prefer, instead, to keep fancying someone for ages before getting regrettably drunk at a work Christmas do, throwing ourselves at his best mate, and living happily ever after.

But chances are you're considering online dating at all because the whole drunken-hookup-as-relationship-starter has not worked out so well for you.

Congratulations. Now take the next logical leap and find out what our American cousins have known all along: it's *fun* to date more than one person at once. Having options when it comes to choosing between men is a *good* thing.

Here are just some of the benefits you can gain from meeting as many potential dates as possible in a short time frame:

* Online dating has an idiotic pricing structure. Buy one month of access, or six? If you meet someone quickly that's just wasted money. Also, as most sites state the date when you joined, this has the potential to look as if you've been left on the shelf that bit too long. Keep it short and sweet.
* If one date goes badly, not to worry! There is no time to dwell on it, with another coming up soon. And you may even be able to wear the same dress again without going to the dry cleaner.
* Men, and this is the sad truth, like to imagine you are in demand and that he will be the one to win you over. So if you are available 'any day in the next fort-night', he won't think too much of how you spend your time.
* You will quickly accumulate a large number of hilarious dating horror stories to tell your friends the next time you get together and be the star of the party.
* If all your first meetings are at coffee bars, be certain to get a loyalty card. Then you can reward yourself with a free latte at the end of the week.

* I personally don't believe in The One. But even if you believe that you could be compatible with perhaps one in a hundred men — or one in a thousand — odds are you probably have to sift through that thousand, yes?

Helpfully, the etiquette of online dating is different from meetings that initiate in 'meat-space' (Nerdish for Real World). It is perfectly acceptable to stop answering someone's contact within the Rule of Three time frame, for instance, if you have not yet met in person. In fact, it is almost expected. The several times I have sent a short, yet polite, note to indicate cessation of my interest it was met with incredulity. Online women, it would seem, prefer just to disappear. Most civilised.

Googling your date before going out, in meat-space, is a topic of much discussion. Is it ethical? Accurate? Informative? Creepy? Worry no longer about new social mores — in online dating land, it is not only acceptable, it's expected.

Daytime dates are also very acceptable. If you have half an hour at lunchtime, and there is a Gregg's nearby — yay, it's a date! Half a pint in the pub closest to your work before you get the bus home? Date. Sharing a sandwich on a park bench? Date, baby. Especially if you are taking full advantage and going on multiple dates in a week, this helps keep running costs to a minimum.

One thing to keep in mind, though, is that online dating will not necessarily be the best way to meet someone to have a relationship with. Random hookups? Hell yes, and then some. Real, lasting love? It can happen, but it is by no means guaranteed.

In fact, studies have shown that people who meet online through interest groups, then start a relationship, are statistically more likely to stay together than couples who met through strictly dating sites. So whether you're a rabid fan of adult-sized squirrel costumes or an active backgammon player, you are far more likely to meet someone suitable for a relationship by getting involved with activities. Meet people online, then meet them in real life, then sit back and wait for sparks to fly. At best you will be introduced to someone, or the friend of someone, with similar interests to yours. At worst you will have a wide network of people in your life who know the perfect dry cleaner for getting difficult stains out of fake fur.

Personally, I think this reflects the offline world rather well. Few people meet their 'soul mates' at quick dating events. Many people meet their partners at functions that bring them together in similar interests. Yeah, it's the old chestnut of not looking for love, but finding it when you least expect it. Your gran was probably right.

As mentioned earlier, one enormous advantage inter-net dating has over almost any other way of meeting people is the possibility that you could very well meet more than one person in whom you are interested. This is good. This is to be encouraged. Or as the saying goes, serial leads to stalking; parallel leads to marriage.

No, I don't know of too many other dating tips that are probably only relevant to electrical engineers. Don't worry.

Anyway, the brilliant thing about dating several men at once if you can pull it off (three being, yet again, the magic number) is that it is a very useful way to assess the range of what you are capable of pulling, and also to compare directly the merits of various men. Rather than measuring their weird quirks and peccadilloes against the sainted memory of The One Who Got Away, you can play their irritating habits off against each other, and in the process, amuse yourself. Brilliant.

So if...	*Then you should...*
Man #1 only ever calls the day before he wants to see you, and you've been keeping your diary clear for him...	Make dates with Men #2 and #3 first. Man #1 will either get the message or fade away.
It's close to Valentine's day and you don't know whom to buy a card for...	Buy for every man you know! Cards are cheaper in bulk packs anyway.

You've made an effort – even been for a waxing – and the date fizzles...	Remember it's never too late to call someone over for a nightcap.
Your bank account is veering dangerously towards the red, and it's only the 15th...	Stack dinner dates for the next week, and make it clear you are a very old-fashioned girl.
You're stuck on a date with a man who is boring you...	Excuse yourself to the ladies' and text the next hottie.

If it horrifies you to think of directing your dating energy at more than one man at a time – the sure sign of a hussy, you believe – remember that men would do the exact same thing given the opportunity. Just because you may be looking for a long-term relationship does not mean you should only date one person at a time – in fact, if that is your goal, you will probably achieve it faster by stacking. So why close yourself off to the possibilities? The first man you meet may be Good Enough, but that is not the point of dating. You do not want Good Enough. You want Better.

Young love yadda yadda. At some point, you will date someone, you will like him, and you will make it exclusive. Congratulations are certainly in order. But should you tell people how you met? Depending on how you have met partners in the past, and the level of geekiness in your extended circle of friends and acquaintances, it might be difficult to overcome the inbuilt aversion to admitting to being one of 'those people' on 'those websites'.

The healthiest tack to take would be to realise that someone else's reaction to your relationship is their problem, not yours. After all they probably met their boyfriend in a drunken fumble in the student union bar toilets circa 2002 so who are they to judge? Reality check: you still care what other people think. So there are different approaches depending on the situation, and of course, your comfort level. In all likelihood your response will fall somewhere on the lie-to-truth continuum:

* *Lie.* 'I spotted him across a crowded room, and without a single word spoken, he came up and kissed me full on the lips...' Cute, charming, and classic — but be certain to get your stories straight first. You don't want him recasting the same fictional meeting as a drunken grope in the copy room.
* *Partial lie (aka evasion).* 'Introduced by a common friend' is a good one. 'Involved in a community group' is another. Technically, both sort of true.

Now cause a diversion by changing the subject. 'Hey, look, are they bringing our meals out now?' Job done. Move along, nothing to see here.

* *Total honesty.* Me and my current paramour met through a Casual Relationships advert I placed on Gumtree*. 'Must be hot in bed' and 'must love Bill Murray' were the main criteria. Honestly. I tell people, they think it's a joke, and the conversation moves swiftly on.

Remember everyone is essentially twelve & you'll be fine

Your best mate in the search for a mate is a good sense of humour and a generous pinch of salt as regards anything people say and do — particularly in the early stages after meeting. This is doubly true for dating people you have met online.

Whatever anyone else might say, the business of meeting people never does get any easier. I say this as someone who met new men all the time — and had to get naked with them approximately five nanoseconds later. You will always feel a little nervous. You will always say or do something that makes you cringe later. Don't be too hard on yourself.

And don't be too hard on them either. Deep down, we are all just a bunch of awkward prepubescents,

---

* Although it is worth mentioning that I was highly sceptical at the start. So much so that I called him a likely rapist and an axe-murderer several times during our first meeting. Happily, he read this as 'charmingly quirky' rather than 'tightly wound ball of neuroses'. Results not typical.

uncertain of whom to sit with at lunch and expecting to be made fools of at any time. Remember that men feel this too, and are usually far, far worse at acknowledging it. So people will sometimes say and do stupid things. Give them some latitude, and don't take everything that happens too much to heart.

CHAPTER 5

How to Be Alluring

— sort your head out first, then your wardrobe

If your approach to meeting Men involves blurry pictures on an agency website, most of the following points are unnecessary. Feel free to skip ahead. If on the other hand you prefer the company of men in longer than one-hour windows, here are a few tips on perfecting the art of being alluring...

Get un-fucked-up already

Seriously, if you are riddled with more self-doubt than the aristocracy has pubic lice, then attraction is going to be a giant stumbling block for you. Men can smell the horror of an emotional mess a mile away — and unlike women, they probably will not steer well clear, at least until they've got sex out of her first. Then they will vacate the premises at speed and with nary a fare-thee-well.

This, in case I have not yet made it clear, is not a desirable situation.

To have a reasonable chance of being in control of any relationship, you need to be in control of your own emotions first. No, this is not the same thing as not having emotions – it means not letting them turn you into the sort of wedding-dress-wearing, mouldering spinster deep inside men always halfway suspect we are anyway. It means knowing appropriate outlets and appropriate limits. It means taking lemons and making the god damned lemonade.

There is an author and – I shudder to use the phrase, but it is appropriate – life coach whose work I greatly admire. His name is Marshall Goldsmith, and he usually focuses on how to make business executives into better people... you know, turning belligerent City directors whose idea of human resources is having the entire executive suite upholstered in the skins of defeated foes into human-like beings, just bearable enough that their entire workforces don't walk out.

What I have learned from his approach is that it really does not matter one bit what the cause of your pain, aggression or general attitude problem is. Disappointing childhood? Join the queue. String of failed relationships? You're not the only one. Awkward cultural background? Honey, I'm Jewish. Cry me a fucking river.

No, it doesn't matter what got you fucked up. You might think it does, and spend decades (not to mention tens of thousands of pounds) in talking therapies of every stripe, dissecting the ins-and-outs of your inner child and why your life and relationships are so fucked up. But in the end, why bother? Why not just change today, and get un-fucked-up already?

Or, to give the concept a little more historical and

philosophical gravitas, there is a well-known saying attributed to Abraham Lincoln that people are usually about as happy as they make up their minds to be.

It is the truth. You, too, are not incapable of happiness. If there is a chemical, physiological reason why you are unhappy, then huzzah, we live in an age where these things can and should be sorted out, thank you very much NHS. And once you have done that, you can just choose to leave the rest behind. Or, to attach some religious gravitas to the concept, do the Buddhist thing and let it go.

Leaving past Man baggage at the door

In the context of romantic relationships, letting things go is often a sticking point for women. *You don't understand*, I can hear you saying right now. *In my last relationship, he was so bad, he...* etc. As if, you know, no one else in the history of womankind ever has had the bad luck to be fettered to a self-centred unfeeling arse.

I assure you, we have all been there. Repeatedly. In every life stage and era of history imaginable. With bells on. Done that. Bought the t-shirt. Bore the mental scars. Parlayed it into a writing career. It is inevitable — after all, if finding a man to love us was so easy, we would all be happily paired off with our first loves. Heartbreak is all but inevitable. Yet somehow people have managed to move on, and so must you.

You know who else I like besides this Goldsmith chap and that dead American president? Minnie Driver. (I know, my taste in cultural influences is impeccable.)

But I was reading an interview with her some time ago that asked about a high-profile breakup, and she shrugged the question off. 'I'm okay,' was her reply. 'Fake it until you make it.' And the topic did not come up again.

That, I thought, is a classy lady. And I don't mean 'classy' in the hooker sense (which usually involves dangly earrings and industrial quantities of eyeliner) either, but an actual woman who is interpreting what happened to her in a reasonable and admirable way. An Ingrid Bergman in *Casablanca*, if you will.

I've no doubt that behind closed doors Ms Driver was hardly as flippant about the situation as all that. I imagine 'I Will Survive', copious amounts of Galaxy and red wine may have been involved. But she had the good sense to realise that to her fans, the forensic details were not important. She realised your thoughts, words, and actions are what you become.

Which leads to the Executive Summary, if you're skimming this bit: Be Ingrid Bergman.

I mean, not in the marrying a louche director sense, but in the calm and collected sense. Have you ever admired the way one of your friends just got on with life after something devastating occurred, such as a death in the family, being made redundant, or breaking a Gina heel in the middle of a date? You can do that too. In fact, you have little choice. Just prioritise the things that are important to you — sorting out the admin, making time for friends and family, locating the gaffa tape — and do them. Set aside some alone time and by all means acknowledge your feelings, but don't allow them to turn you into a blubbering mess.

Crucially, men are somewhat more observant than we give them credit for. In fact they would almost have to be, or risk being biologically reclassified as protozoa. If you are seeking companionship strictly in order to fill a hole in your life left by the last man, he may not be able to put his finger on it, but he will sense something is wrong and pull away. At speed. Similarly, if your previous experiences have so embittered you to men in general that you interpret everything he says and does through the lens of what your lying, cheating, good-for-sod-all ex said and did, he will resent that and pull away. For all the bluster and bravado, Men are really skittish little things, and your anger scares the Bird's custard out of them.

You're a woman, damn it. You will not be shattered into tiny pieces by stupid boys and the things they say and do. You are better than that.

...and eventually, with enough practice, that will become your truth.

Effective coping strategies

At the same time, it is important to take note of a significant advantage we women have over men — the ability to acknowledge our feelings — and use that in a positive manner. When a man inadvertently feels something, he usually crushes it into a little ball, puts it in the pit of his stomach, and piles food, beer and anabolic steroids on top of it.

We, on the other hand, like to share. Copiously.

Talking isn't a bad thing as such, but there can be something truly off-putting about the woman who mistakes having lots of feeling with being in touch with her feelings.

I'm not just talking about from the dating perspective, incidentally. No one enjoys treading the same ground with you over and over again with no solution in sight. Much as I adore my friend R, I know if she rings it's not because she is actually interested in my life, or sharing the good things about hers, but in telling me about yet *another* date gone terribly, irretrievably wrong. And I get tense and tetchy as a result. Usually she will come around eventually to seeing the funny or practical side of a rubbish situation, but until then, it's all 'he-said-this-what-should-I-think?' nonsense. Yes, friends are the ones who should be there for you no matter what, but don't abuse that privilege.

So how to strike a useful balance between denying your feelings, and paralysing your life with them? Here is a cut-and-keep guide:

* In the privacy of your own home, or in a locked toilet cubicle at work, acknowledge your feelings. Cry if you must.
* Talk to a friend if you can, but keep the call under three hours. Seriously. We are not all on the same contract as you, and that shit don't come cheap.
* Go do a displacement activity – exercise is brilliant for this. Sex is also recommended, though of course preferably with a FB whose services you have

already secured, not one you are pursuing now out of desperation.

* Enjoy the resulting endorphin high. If endorphin is not forthcoming, invest in a modest amount of quality drink. Treat yourself to something you would not ordinarily buy for yourself.

* Suitably well-oiled, find a nearby mirror and repeat potentially embarrassing self-esteem mantras such as: I am a good person, and I deserve a nice life.

* Have a good old laugh about how pathetic that all sounds, resolve to pull yourself together instead, and get back out there lady!

* If anyone asks about your recent woe, simply smile enigmatically and change the subject. The less you say, the more your forbearance will be admired. You may even get a few drinks bought for you in the process.

Be interesting

Quick quiz 1: You meet a man who is potential relationship material. How would you rank these qualities of his in terms of importance?

☐ *Gym-honed pecs and stylish hair*
☐ *Large income and expensive taste*
☐ *Positive attitude and fun demeanour*
☐ *A wide range of interests and things to talk about or do*

It doesn't take a genius to see that for the most part the first two will rank rather lower than the latter two. Unless of course your idea of a great relationship is hanging out with the glam but dim, and learning to forgo the finer points of, you know, conversation.

Quick quiz 2: Rank these feminine traits in order of desirability to men:

☐ *Elaborate hair and makeup*
☐ *Large income and expensive taste*
☐ *Positive attitude and fun demeanour*
☐ *A wide range of interests and things to talk about or do*

Hey, surprise, the answers for what men want are pretty similar to the answers for what you want. And yet, when women talk about making an effort for a man, nine times out of ten this involves some permutation of the frantic last-minute haircut/tanning booth/shopping/manicure montage.

Men are visual creatures, without doubt, and good personal grooming habits are always appreciated – but let's not credit them with more eyeball than brain. They crave passionate nonsexual mental stimulation just as much as we do, in spite of the implication otherwise that *Nuts et al.* are doing a stellar job of perpetuating. It would be an exceptionally shallow man who values the superficial over the substantial, and that probably is not someone you would want to be with anyway, right?

Right??

Anyway, provided you answered *of course not! I have some vestigial self respect* to that question, then consider, next time your date-night preparations involve a preening regime which covers approximately the same length of the time it takes to turn coal into diamonds, whether at least some small fraction of that might be better spent – ooh I don't know – picking up a newspaper or something.

Having interests translates as confidence to do and be things on your own without expecting a man to do and be for you. And confidence is attractive. Not to mention independence.

If you don't give a man something to like about you apart from the superficial things, chances are, he won't stick around long – if he even notices you at all. And frankly, aspiring to achieve WAG-tastic levels of arm candiness is *so* last millennium.

Be interested

What turns men off? When they get the distinct feeling that they're being auditioned for a role, not appreciated as individuals.

I know, again with the 'men and women really having loads in common' shocker.

So, how to let a fellow know you're considering his particular merits, not just whether he could squeeze into a DJ and manage not to trip up on his way to the altar? By being genuinely curious about his life, his thoughts, his interests.

It is unbelievably appealing when the person you are talking to seems to be genuinely interested in what you have to say rather than just waiting their turn to speak. So if you've met a man who inspires this feeling in you, by all means return the favour. Ask him about himself and really listen to the answers.

This doesn't mean you need to start mirroring him. 'Oh, you love *Star Trek*-themed bouldering! I've always been fascinated by that, I'll go and get an Uhura dress tomorrow...' No, that's a bit too far on the side of The Crazy.

In fact, even if the gent in question is not someone you care to meet up with again, still be interested. See what you can learn — people can miss a lot when they are only listening to glean the bits they want to pay attention to rather than hearing the full context. By not just turning off into the smile-and-nod, you might discover something useful, such as: is this someone who is not dating material, but might be appropriate for someone I know? Could we be friends? Can I learn something about how to avoid these idiots in future? Will he eventually say his address, thus making filing an official complaint with the police far easier?

Men only want one thing... unconditional acceptance

Some say they're breast men; others claim to prefer a long leg or a pleasing backside. These, I hope you've realised, are details. What a man really and truly craves is someone who loves him for who he is, and is not on a mission to change that.

But! But! I can hear you say. *You haven't seen this one! His clothes/boutique facial hair/irritating best mate/poor taste in lager! If only I could make that one thing different, he would be perfect!*

This is the trap of being a modern woman, I'm afraid. So accustomed are we to the idea that with sufficient time and effort, any situation can be mastered, that we fail to see how this is a limiting and damaging way to view other people.

Turn the situation on its head. Let us imagine that, four dates in, Mr Perfect tells you that you are every inch the woman for him, apart from the fact that you are blonde, not brunette.

What does the sensible woman do? Tick the answer closest to your initial instinct:

- ☐ *Procure pornographic images of attractive blondes in order to make her case*
- ☐ *Go directly to the salon the next morning for a session with the colourist*
- ☐ *Laugh and tell him if he doesn't like it, too bad*
- ☐ *Do nothing, apart from starting to silently resent all dark-haired women everywhere*

If you ticked the third choice, well done! That is exactly the response he should get to such a ludicrous request.

However, so unaccustomed are modern men to laughing in our faces, that the female equivalent ('Sweetness, I would love you but that mole on your chin must go') is rarely met with the public disdain it deserves. Instead he either chooses to ignore your request – thus leading to insanely bottomless levels of resentment on your side – or to try to conform, which only serves to reinforce the lesson that your nagging will give the desired result – which leads to, well, more nagging.

Hey, if that floats your soap, don't let me stop you.

In my previous relationships, I was the Queen of

Nag. Someone cooked an egg the wrong way? Disaster! A boyfriend turned out to be the sort of person who would circle a car park for hours selecting the perfect spot rather than going for the nearest available one and getting on with life? Apocalypse!

It was only many years (and failed relationships) later that I learned the golden rule of dating, and in fact, getting by with other people in general:

You are just as annoying as everyone else in the world.

Wait, what?

Yes, it is in fact true that no one is perfect, and the time you've spent wondering why everyone else in the world is such an idiot was, in fact, time everyone else was spending wondering the exact same about you because you were doing annoying things right back without even realising it.

You thought:	*You were actually:*
You were a decent, inoffensive person without even trying.	Being exactly as offensive as everyone around you.
You were getting even with irritating people by being irritable yourself, but to nowhere near the level they were.	Being an irritating ultra-arse who escalated the situation far past where it should have been.
You were trying hard to be a kind, easy-to-get-on-with person.	Being only mildly irritating to everyone else.
You were making insane, over-the-top, conciliatory, and helpful gestures to all family, friends, and strangers you came into contact with.	Doing a decent impersonation of an actual nice person.

Hit me like a diamond bullet, that realisation did. All the times I had been bothering this or that poor boy into 'correcting' his 'faults', I had in fact been nurturing my own like hothouse tomatoes. And my, were they large and juicy. As it turned out I wasn't perfect after all —shocking I know — but people had been accepting of my idiosyncrasies because, well, it's a matter of learning to take people on their own terms or risk turning into either an agoraphobic curtain-twitcher writing indignant letters to the *Sunday Times* or a mass murderer with gleaming rifles swinging out from under your Matrix-style leather duster (your choice). And if I am being completely honest, neither sounds a very attractive option, either mentally or sartorially.

So, how to live with the loveable quirks and foibles that so quickly will become the grit in the Vaseline of your relationship?

It is a fairly straightforward thing, in fact: ask yourself whether with a little bit of friendly patience you can live with this particular habit/facial hair arrangement/ religious cult, unchanged, forever?

If the answer is...	*Then...*
Yes	Get over it already and don't make a production out of it. Shouldn't you be spending your time more productively on things that actually matter?
No	Get out of the relationship, stat, and don't make a production out of it. Shouldn't you be spending your time more productively looking for your real Mr Right?

Leave them wanting more

(This page intentionally left blank)

How to dress

Before I forget, the outside part: in order for a man to discover your inner beauty, you want to attract him in the first place i.e. you want to look good as well. Oh, let me guess. You Don't Play Games. You think a man (or indeed anyone else for that matter) should love you in all your long armpit-hair, dowdy gym kit, granny knickered glory.

You're right. He should. But he won't. Not at first, anyway.

On the one hand, there really is no lack of resources for instruction for women on how to do so. We're all but drowning in tips for applying liquid eyeliner. But when all is said and done, there are a few general tips you should probably keep in mind just the same. I'll leave the specific details to the glossies. First, let us begin with the *Don'ts*:

Never let a man catch you in...	*Because...*
Ugg Boots, Crocs and the rest	I don't understand the point of these and neither do men. If you need wellies, buy wellies. If you need slippers, buy slippers. Do not wander the high street in anything serving the same purpose as wellies or slippers. It is simple, and yet, we have made it complicated. The madness must stop.

Hooker minis	I'm a hooker, and not even I have a crotch-skimming mini. If you require something that short, consider hot-pants. But anything that causes the casual observer to wonder whether it's a belt or a skirt is best left to the pages of *Maxim*. And they make your upper thighs look horrendous, I'm sorry to report.
Plaits	Practical, childish, ever-so-slightly hockey team. Not a fantastic combination in a desirable female. And if your man specifically requests these... I for one would lose his number. Fast.
Body glitter	Want to leave him with a subtle reminder of your presence after you've gone? Shitting the bed would be more subtle, not to mention more easily washed out.
Excessive perfume	The jury may still be out on whether humans have as primal a response to their lovers' pheromones as other animals do, but one thing is for certain, no species on earth has yet to be shown to be uncontrollably attracted to bucketloads of Britney Spears' *Curious*.

For every *Don't* there must be a *Do*; so here they are:

You really should consider...	*Because...*
Skirts (of the non-hooker variety)	No one ever asked 'does my bum look big in this?' when in a skirt. Fact. Not even the Edwardians – they went so far as to add padding to the backside, don't you know. Skirts make your arse look feminine and your legs look great.
Minimal makeup	Everyone knows a tragic girl who has natural beauty but on a night out manages to magically transform into a circus sideshow. Don't be that girl. Also don't believe men who say they prefer 'no makeup' – they don't know what that looks like. What they mean is smooth skin, bright eyes and glossy lips. Which we all know is more easily achievable through cosmetics than genetics.
Great underwear	...that fits properly. I know, everyone bangs on about it. But even the most gorgeous dress can be ruined by a sagging décolletage, and there simply is no excuse. It will lift your confidence, as well.

Moderate heel height	Screw trends. They exist to make you look stupid. Add height and elongate the leg, by all means, but not so much you are incapable of standing in a taxi queue much less running for the bus.
Manicures	See minimal makeup, above. No need for red talons – but looking down at a pair of feminine hands is nice for everyone involved. Plus it gives you reason to suggest he does the washing up tonight.

CHAPTER 6

Care and Feeding

— a guide to long-term maintenance of your new pet

N ow let us get to the part where you have successfully identified and tagged a man, and taken him
back to your enclosure for long-term study. What now?

Though capable of obtaining many of their basic
needs for themselves, it is nonetheless generally agreed
that a woman's touch may enhance the quality of a
Man's habitus. However, a word of caution: as with
young children and dogs, Men are quick to spoil.
Never feed him from the table, never let him break the
rules, and most importantly of all, never EVER allow
him to take you for granted. A firm but loving hand is
key to success...

Sex: being the best he's ever had —
you'll never see this in Cosmo

There's a reason there isn't more pornography geared
towards women, and it's not because women don't like
sex. It's because when it comes to what pushes the
buttons, there is a fundamental disjunction between
what does it for men and what does it for women.

So when you're imagining...	*He's actually thinking...*
A few lit candles will set the mood nicely. I bet he'll love these scented ones.	Shit, she's put the lights off again, I can't see her tits!
A few more pillows and throws strewn across the bed will make it a more inviting place to play.	Crap, she's only gone and put *more* stuff in the way. Have to shift operations to the dining table again.
If we read erotic poetry aloud together, that would be a real turn-on.	Oh no, what am I, at school again? I hope there isn't going to be a quiz after this.
He'll love this new lingerie set, a snip at 200 quid.	Nice gift wrapping. Now where is the good stuff?

The bottom line is that while we are spending a lot of time engineering the getting-to-sex point, he is spending a lot of time focused on the actually-having-sex part.

Some years ago I happened into a conversation with the owner of a chain of successful strip clubs. They were known for their attractive, one might almost venture to say respectable, environs: tastefully lit and decorated, large dressing rooms for the girls, modern advertising aimed at a more discerning customer.

And what did the successful entrepreneur have to say regarding the effect of his semi-sanitised clubs on the men? That they had no effect on the men — if you put naked ladies in a shed, men would pay to see it – but it did serve to attract the more in-demand female performers.

The luxe wrapping at his club was for the girls, not the clients.

Which is not to say that men have no appreciation for the finer points of presentation – after all, there exists a market for call girls in a world where £10 street-walkers are also found in abundance – but that it simply isn't as much a priority for them as it is for us. And if anything is to be learned from the story of the strip club owner it is that each sex can benefit from better understanding of what appeals to the other.

Not to worry, I'm not going to bore you with all the shite about how prehistoric man liked rape in forests vs. prehistoric women valued picking shiny berries and scattering animal skins around the cave. Whether by accident or design, women respond to sex and imagery differently than men do, and the point is not whether nature or nurture is to blame, but rather what to do about it.

Ironically the solution is not to approximate the blonde, bikini'ed bimbo of a thousand gross-out teen films. While on paper a perfect ten with a beer in each hand might seem appealing to a man – and probably would be, for a single night – looking the part and easy availability make for great stories to swap with his mates, but not necessarily great sex. (And in case the point needs reiterating – you want to be having great, regular sex more often than you are turning up in pub anecdotes.) In other words, having good sex is not about the set dressing, be it gauzy curtains and music on low, or straight-up banging in a pub toilet. Good sex happens when you use your head, and credit the man with the ability to recognise that imagination is the most powerful asset in your sexual arsenal. Particularly once you've been together for longer than a few weeks.

I've said it before but it bears repeating: what is the secret to the prefect blowjob? Two things — saliva and enthusiasm. You read that right. Enthusiasm. Not *saliva and perfect makeup*. Not *saliva and a home-cooked meal*. Not even *saliva and the ability to deep-throat something the approximate dimensions of your forearm* (though truth be told that wouldn't hurt). Enthusiasm is the key. No window dressing in the world could possibly make up for the fact that when you are in bed with a man, the things he wants most is to imagine he's rocking your world to its very foundation, and you don't do that with red lacy briefs and porn acting. You do that by genuinely forgetting about the rest of the world for a bit and living in the moment.

So let us generalise the concept:

∞

The secret to great sex is enthusiasm

∞

Maybe it sounds retrograde to you? Quite possibly when making your list of nonnegotiable traits in a lover, your enthusiasm did not come into consideration so much as rarefied concepts like respect and consideration. And while those are jolly good things, they have no place in the bedroom.

Hot sex consists of going to bed with someone you respect and admire and forgetting, at least for a short time, about the respect and admiration part. Because getting into the moment is hot; moment by moment paranoia about whether he will still regard you intellectually once he's seen you in every compromising position and a few you didn't even know you were flexible enough for, a bit less so.

Cooking: the way to a man's heart is through his...

It has been said that a man wants a whore in the bedroom, and a chef in the kitchen. True?

Yes and no. Boiled down to its essential elements, this advice re: keeping a relationship on form consists of these points:

* Keep his balls empty
* Keep his stomach full

But you needn't be the Hostess with the Mostest to fulfil these criteria.

Don't fool yourself into believing that in order to bag and keep a fellow you are required to provide Cordon Bleu-standard nosh at every opportunity. Attempting to do so creates a number of problems, all of them unattractive:

* What if your cooking isn't up to scratch? Then he

will feel forced to be polite, and resent you.
* What if he thinks the cooking is fine, but you spend the entire time undermining yourself with 'oh, my cooking is usually better than this. It's so over-salted...' leading him to wonder exactly what variety of neurotic you are?
* What if you spent all your time preparing the meal, and by the time that was finished, were too tired for sex?
* What if you cook so well, and so often, that he comes to expect it, thereby rendering any special effort in that department useless?

As fate would have it I might have been blessed with a modicum of sexual sense, but when it comes to the domestic niceties I'm the Hostess with Not So Much. But there has rarely been cause for complaint about the level of service around my flat, largely because I have benefitted from sticking to a few rules:

1.) Men like to provide. Therefore, make him feel more of a man by telling him to make you break-fast.
2.) House rules are, whomever cooks breakfast does the washing up.
3.) As he was so sweet as to provide you with susten-ance for the day, the food arrangements for future nights in will be arranged by you, why, you'll even do the washing up...
4.) ...which means keeping a wide selection of deliv-ery and takeaway menus to hand and dispatching the empties straight into the bin. Job done!

Is it really that simple? Yes, it really is. Remember, most men spend the years between being flung from the comforting arms of Mummy's cooking and bagging a wife, in the company of a microwave and Pot Noodle. And what's better, when you do crack out the mad skills and whip up the perfect Sunday roast (some six months in, at a minimum) he's well positioned to declare you a bona fide domestic goddess.

Domestic arrangements:
your space, your money, your life

Have you ever been guilty of any of the following:

* Left your hairclips/toothbrush/underwear at a man's house in order to have a reason to go back?
* Manufactured ways to make certain it's far too late for you not to stay over (or vice versa)?
* Demanded a drawer, shelf, or other allocation of space in his flat without it being suggested first?
* 'Accidentally' dropped something of his (phone charger, Oyster card) into your handbag, so he would have a reason to come and see you?
* Rearranged – or imagined rearranging – your furniture to accommodate his things when the topic of moving in has not even been broached yet?

If you answered 'yes' to three or more, then you have a clear case of Domestic Borderline Disorder (DBD).

If such a disease actually existed – and let us remember that they all existed before they were accepted by the medical establishment, people – it would be characterised by a serious, overwhelming, and inappropriate need to intermingle your belongings with a man's.

What makes DBD such a dangerous diagnosis, you might wonder. Especially when, for most women and even the odd man here and there, the end goal of dating is to eventually merge everything from genitals to household items to genetic material.

Let us revisit the principal principle of dating: that until a firm commitment is made, all parties are free to change their minds. Which means breakups can and do happen at any time with no notice. But if you've been an adopter of early and aggressive commingling, what would otherwise be the short, sharp shock of breakup becomes a long, drawn-out affair in which the provenance of certain DVDs is discussed and haggled over. Endlessly.

Now Belle, I can hear you argue, *there is no need to take such an aggressively pessimistic viewpoint. After all, going in with negative assumptions about outcome can be a hindrance to relationship-building*. And you'd be right.

But there is a fine line between pessimism and being realistic, and having a healthy balance of realism in mind can only be a good thing. Plus, it is important to many men to feel they are being chosen, not chased; letting him suggest major decisions such as sharing a sock drawer can help to establish (in his mind, even if you've long since come to the same conclusion) that he is the one pushing you for commitment, not the other way round. So when he suggests moving in together: fantastic! Break out the boxes and packing tape you have had ready all along. Until then, they are just 'left over from my last move'.

Money presents similar problems, and the dynamics change over time within a couple. Past relationships have thrown up a lot of issues regarding money, here are just a few things regarding men and money I had to learn the hard way:

* If you're a hooker, take the Tube when out with your (lower-earning) boyfriend. Don't suggest a black cab. Ever.
* Let him book the holiday on his cards, then pay him back. That way if he cancels you're not the one stuck taking your mother on a romantic Parisian city break.
* Try not to talk about tax rates. It's just fucking boring and no one cares.
* Don't suggest your accountant to your boyfriend. If he takes your advice he'll feel henpecked; if he doesn't you'll feel he has something to hide.
* If you spent more on shoes/booze/condoms and lube in any given month than you did on rent, for pity's sake keep this to yourself.
* Never ask him to sit outside a client's house as your security. It doesn't matter if you offer him a cut of the take or not.

Here is my advice on the subject, with the caveat that as the eldest, I never properly learned to share.

Early stage relationships

On the first few dates, the convention is the man pays. But when you've got to the stage of going on mini-breaks together, or nights out become a regular thing, what then? Should he always pick up the tab?

My advice would be no, but introduce your own finances slowly. Even if you make loads more than the man he is not entitled to a lion's share of it. Discretion is a good idea here — you wouldn't want to end up saddled with the XY equivalent of a gold-digger — as well as a certain amount of fluffing of the male ego. He works hard; taking you out is his reward. And it would be a pity to deprive him of the pleasure of enjoying that, no?

However, just as I have no tolerance for the sort of woman who is incapable of opening a car door herself, there is no sense in carrying things on to the point where he starts to imagine you might be taking advantage of him. After a few dates, if he pays for the meal, you cover the taxis; if he books the minibreak, you pay for the day spa.

Late stage relationships

As long as they were together — 25+ years married — my parents never had a joint bank account. Never. And there was never a single argument about money between them. Everything else in the world, yes, absolutely. But they never rowed over who should pay in what amount to whatever.

Because their careers progressed at different paces, and because my father changed jobs more often than my mother did, it was impossible to calculate a ratio either of them 'should' be contributing. So when the bills arrived, they simply had a conversation about who should cover what – 'I'll do the mortgage this time if you do the utilities' – and that was that.

In other words, they communicated. Like grown-ups.

The problem where money is involved is that situations rarely remain static, but the convention of a joint account does not take this into, erm, account. You might pay in different amounts, but with one partner feeling more entitled than the other to withdrawals, or someone expecting equality in all things even if you're making more than twice what he is.

That isn't to say people can't have adult, rational discussions where paying into the community chest is involved. But when you keep track of your own money, there is less taking for granted. And also it gives a level of independence that women have worked hard to win. I wouldn't be in a rush to hand it over so quickly.

Then again, I could be wrong. Your mileage, as the saying goes, might vary.

And of course no discussion of independence would be complete without touching on the topic of your extracurricular interests (no, not the sexy ones... unless of course you are *that* sort of couple).

Long-term considerations

Relationships, and the maintenance thereof, are a careful balancing act. Initial attraction relies on a physical connection. Dating is usually the result of having something in common. And long-term relationships only really last when the people involved have similar attitudes and values. So in order to maintain something good, something that works, you should be looking for – and hopefully working together at – all three levels.

But who cares about that rubbish? The big question is really 'when, and to what extent, can I let myself go?'

Don't pretend you don't. I know I do. Hell, that was one of the perks of being a call girl: in the off times, I allowed myself to be as slovenly as possible without even so much as a hint that some man would come walking through and be horrified by the sight of what he previously thought was a, if not beautiful, at least passably well-groomed woman.

But obviously once someone starts hanging around your place for more than one hour a week, you start to think about how you can manage him seeing you without having to go through the over-the-top preparation on a daily basis. So on some level, you must consider how, and to what extent, to let him in on how you really are.

This depends mainly on just how much of what the man saw in the first place was an idealised version of you. In the first few months, did you shave every day, only to find your crotch stubble could now double as a useful sanding block? Were you going for twice-weekly acrylic extensions in porn star-tastic French manicure for six weeks, only to belatedly discover the real nails underneath had given up and fallen off? Has he never seen you in daylight so you can slip out of the re-inforced-tum control pants unnoticed? Did you tell him you spoke six languages, had a master's from Oxford, and travelled the world as a freelance translator to the stars, but are afraid he's one overnight stay from discovering the NatWest pussy-bow blouse at the bottom of your clothes hamper?

If so, then you are faced with three options, which are almost always type-specific:

Are you a... *Scary Bitch?* Come clean on the real colour of your hair/length of your nails/proportions of your backside, and face the consequences for good or for ill.

> *Pros:* Probably the most time-saving approach.
> *Cons:* Who knew he was only dating you because he though you were an ex-circus performer? Men, eh.

Are you a... *Good Girl?* Book a girls' fortnight away in Spain, change everything back to normal, and on return claim 'What do you mean? It's always been this way!'

> *Pros:* He probably can't actually remember and will go along with whatever you say.
> *Cons:* You will need to go and surreptitiously prune your previous holiday snaps, online profiles, and so on before he catches on.

Are you a... *Plain Jane?* Keep up the pretence forever.

> *Pros:* He will continue to imagine you as the unsullied pinnacle of female perfection.
> *Cons:* He will continue to imagine you as the unsullied pinnacle of female perfection.

If, on the other hand, you conducted yourself with a reasonable measure of honesty — and let's be honest, no one is completely honest when dating, and anyone who says so is lying — then you have a lot less to back-track later. The odd slip-up can be easily reclassified as an imperfect memory (yours or his, depending). The man will probably see right through this. Not to worry — he will probably be too polite to mention it, and in no small part relieved that he now has some justification for 'clearing up' a few of his own lies as well.

On the delicate subject of sex in a long-term relationship, opinions diverge wildly as to the correct course of action. While it is a simple matter to convince your fella that you are a raging, five-times-a-night sex machine when it's early days and he only sees you once a week anyway (the day you shaved, right?) keeping up the action is rather more of a challenge when the days become weeks, months, years...

A quick survey of female friends and acquaintances uncovered a wealth of suggestions about how to address the problem of divergent sex drives:

* Be away with work. Often.
* Work night jobs.
* Have a baby, preferably several.
* Tell him you come harder when it's only once a week.
* Tell him you think it's hot when he masturbates in the shower alone.
* Sneak sleeping pills into his evening meal.
* Change religion and claim he can't touch you until he converts.

* Pull the 'you only want me for sex' crying guilt-trip.
* Tell him he looks like his dad when he comes.
* Tell him he looks like your dad when he comes.
* Feign a perversion so unusual and complex that having sex at all requires twelve weeks' planning (n.b.: he might go for this anyway).
* Claim your period actually comes for two weeks, every fortnight.
* Claim a fake 'female problem'.

Personally, I tend to think having actual sex is probably more time-efficient than most of these strategies. But as always, your results may vary.

N.B.: Once you relax your standards with a man, you will be on very shaky ground regarding his faults. While it might seem to you that cessation of daily blowjobs is hardly on the same level as releasing gas in bed that would raise corpses from the grave, as pointed out extensively in earlier chapters the Man's mind works rather differently to our own, and in cases of propriety and hygiene this is particularly the case. Consider yourself warned.

CHAPTER 7

Setting It Free

— breakups and other endings

Turning him down

They say if you love something to set it free. Curiously, this is also the recommended strategy for when you do *not* love something. I'm certain there are probably good biology-based reasons why pushing away manages both to attract and repel the opposite sex. And why Sting would write a song about such. But ours is not to question why. Ours is to question how.

Part of the art of being successfully single is knowing when to remain so. There is no point to being happy in your own company if you're going to give that up just because some man indicated he might like to have you around for the occasional sex once a week until he gets bored of you and moves on. No, it is imperative that you remain in control at all times.

Part of this comes from acknowledging what it is you really are seeking in a relationship — hopefully you considered this circa Chapter 1; if not, I'll wait while you refresh your memory.

Get it? Got it? Good.

Now, just because you found someone interesting enough to make initial contact — maybe he smelled nice, or didn't remind you too much of your father, or casually dropped a mention of his father's estate in Skye into the first conversation — but for whatever reason, you would like to experience more. Only, once you do, you find out that first wave of chemical attraction is perhaps not going to be enough...

Before a first meeting: CTRL-ALT-DEL

It is entirely acceptable just to disappear at this point. Really. I know you Good Girls were probably raised to be ladylike, with the most beautiful of manners, but trust me... engaging in the whys and wherefores of how the attraction is not happening for you is a waste of your time. Also, he will probably try to talk you into meeting anyway. Don't fall for this Jedi mind trick men play — 'How do you know you won't like me, if you won't see me?' Plain Janes, I'm looking in *your* direction. Any man who would stoop so low is childish, irritating, and best avoided altogether, really.

If somewhere between making initial contact and getting together for latte *à deux* you've lost that loving feeling, but haven't the *cojones* to say it straight, just lose his number. Lose it. And if you happen to encounter the lad again and he doesn't blank you, smile politely and keep moving. It is in everyone's best interests.

Sat across a table, ten minutes into a date, and suddenly it hits you. Not the particular colour of his eyes, not the dapper way he holds a fork. But. Oh. My. God. Has there ever been a man less interesting in the history of the world, ever? Hopefully you've been clever enough to set up some sort of signal with a trusted friend – you make your excuses, disappear to the loo and text 'colossal bore' (um, we all know by now not to text at the table, yes?). She phones back in five minutes with some invented emergency you *simply must* leave the date to attend to *right now*. Be certain to make it the sort of emergency where a man would be useless, or you might find yourself being escorted to a nonexistent fire by Mr Have-a-Go Hero – better to say she's just been dumped, or is experiencing mysterious 'lady problems' only another woman could comprehend.

And if you have not taken such a precaution, or all your girlfriends are busy, then perhaps you've taken the alternative route of making clear your packed schedule includes another activity planned for straight after. Though it is important to be careful here – don't give away too many details of what you might be doing next, and don't make it anything he could conceivably invite himself along to.

Otherwise you, too, may experience this horror: I had made a mistake of meeting a man for drinks once and letting him know I was meeting other friends later at a pub down the road. When he turned out, surprisingly enough, to be instant Sahara on the erotic potential front, I made my excuses. But guess who 'happened' to drop in to the pub and walk up to me and my mates not an hour later? Exactly. Be busy, but mysterious. If, on the other hand, it happens to be going well and you really want to see more of him, you can drag him along or change your plans.

After a first date: Try anything once (but not twice)

Short of ignoring someone you 'met' online, this is probably the easiest and most natural time to reject someone, because they can't possibly argue that you haven't given them a chance. Easiest for you, that is. He no doubt will have imagined all sorts of possible futures, what colour dresses his friends would wear at your wedding, what your children together would look like...

Okay, no. But be prepared for a small amount of disappointment.

My mother, bless her, would be appalled if she knew I was telling you how to dump someone after a single date. This is not her style. She is, after all, the same woman who once told me, after a disastrous first date involving his 'accidental' forgetting of a wallet followed swiftly by my 'accidental' forgetting of a PIN number, that I should definitely accept a second invitation because what if I had been wrong the first time? As far as advice goes the 'try anything twice' maxim is a relatively sound approach to life – your sex life in particular – but there are exceptions to every rule and I believe heroin and terrible dates count as decent exceptions to this one.

So if you find yourself having to do the deed after one date, stick to the simple truth – 'You're nice but not for me. Good luck,' and leave it at that. DO NOT offer to be friends. DO NOT offer to set him up with friends of yours. Cut him loose and let him fly free; he's a grown-up and so are you. Lies do not suit grown-ups.

So the key is, keep it short, sweet, and on the phone. Email is acceptable if you met or mainly communicated in electronic format. Don't arrange to meet in person before breaking the news; he'll think you've just made a second date and that he is well in there. And don't leave it too long after the first date, either – about two days is good, long enough to show you've had a serious think, short enough that he hasn't asked you out again already. Because you didn't agree to a second date at the end of the first, right? Right?!?

After several dates: The Stalker Zone

Now things start to get a touch more difficult. Partly because a man, by the third date, might be expecting a little action and to get a rejection instead – not just of sex, but everything about him – is vastly ego-shattering; partly because it's impossible for you to do this one by ignoring or over email.

When my friends and I compared notes, we agreed that part of what makes rejection at this point so tricky is that it is a real danger area – the interval where if someone is going to express his stalkerish tendencies, he will. Between dates two and five you are officially in the Stalker Zone and must tread very carefully indeed. If someone knows you for less than a few dates and you call time, he usually won't take it personally; longer than that (i.e. an actual relationship), and he'll be sick enough of your shit to want to see the back of you. But after a few dates he might well be hooked and go stupid on you. And while it's never a good idea, should the rejection seem to be taking a frightening turn, to explicitly state a desire to involve the police, it is always worth remembering that this is what they do for a living, and to keep your phone fully charged.

Rejecting a man by phone is just about still acceptable here, especially if he rings you to set up the next date, but I'm afraid it is getting into the territory where only a face-to-face chat will do. Preferably in daytime hours and in a casual setting where you can get away quickly.

Just as unfortunately it is almost *de rigeur* at this point to offer to be someone's friend instead. However, this is a myth. You don't have to be friends with anyone you don't genuinely regard as solid friendship material, and what's more, he will probably see this for the skimpy line it is and think badly of you. No — just be straightforward.

And if straightforward doesn't appear to be working, then claim you've met someone else. Then walk away quickly. And change your number.

But... but... it's complicated!

If you've been with someone for longer than a few dates, and it is not explicitly a fuck-buddy arrangement, then you can tell whatever lies you want, but you're dating. Fact. Which means when it ends, it will be just like any relationship ending, even if you never once called him your boyfriend.

How, exactly, does one learn when to hold 'em and when to fold 'em? Knowing whether a problem you are experiencing in a relationship is worth breaking up over is subject to a lot of discussion in the various self-help manuals. Entire agony aunt careers have been focused on this very question. Films have been made; series aired. You would think that, as women, we would have this bit sorted, or at least a sizeable wealth of collective wisdom to fall back on.

Alas, that is not the case. We are shit at ending things, because we hate to disappoint people. It isn't what *nice girls* do. So we try to patch things up, or talk it out with our friends... anything to avoid the inevitable. But what you need is not more discussion — what you need is a simple, cut-and-keep heuristic that will clearly indicate whether a situation is worth saving... or whether it's time to stop throwing good effort after bad.

That's why I use this simple, mathematical approach to deciphering drama: the *Dear Deidre Equation*.

Have you ever considered writing to a columnist to ask for advice, only to find yourself stymied by the fact that your particular situation is so complex, the individual details so important, that there is no way to fit it all on a single side of A4? When you talk to your friends about the problems in your love life, has the barman called time before you've even got to the question? Then my friend, what you need is liberal application of the Dear Deidre Equation.

Love situations can look confusing on the surface, but often by breaking them down into their component people and situations they can be clearly assessed in a logical, and dare I say it mathematical, manner.

Take this situation: Alice has been friends with Ben for yonks and had a crush on him the entire time. Ben is holding a torch for Cherry, but Cherry is hung up over married lover Daniel. Alice and Ben start dating and Alice is over the moon. A few months in she has a pregnancy scare and Ben isn't 100% supportive, but she doesn't think twice about it. Married man Daniel is moving with his work to another country, and because his family are not going along, Cherry is considering following.

One night, Alice accidentally reads an email exchange between Ben and Cherry in which he admits that the pregnancy scare would not have bothered him if he was really in love with Alice (which he isn't). In fact he admits his love for Cherry and begs her not to move. Cherry says she is torn between him and Daniel. Alice shouldn't have looked at his email, obvs, but now that she knows — now what? She's angry because she feels Ben broke her confidence about the pregnancy scare. She's sad that he says he doesn't love her, and her instinct is telling her that the situation is wrong. 'But it's not as simple as that,' she thinks. 'It's so *complicated*. There is so much going on here, so many factors. No one else in the history of ever has experienced exactly what I am going through right now so knowing what to do is impossible.' Whatever will she do?

This is a job for the *Dear Deidre Equation*!

First you count up the number of people involved (x), keeping in mind that in any interpersonal interaction there are in fact four sides to every individual to be considered (4x):

* The person you think you are
* The person he thinks he is
* The person he thinks you are
* The person you think he is

and so on.

And if Alice imagines her situation is unique and therefore merits a different set of rules to anyone else's relationship, unfortunately, she is mistaken. Of course people have experienced what she is experiencing right now — and often worse. But we are all convinced that our particular details make the ending different, somehow. They don't. But it can be difficult to discern that when you're in Dear Deidre territory.

The most straightforward way for Alice to figure out if she should extricate herself from the relationship is to add up the potential number of independent agony aunt questions within the relationship, each of length 4x:

1. Daniel

* Cheating on his wife (Daniel + wife = x = 2)
* Dragging his mistress to another country to continue the infidelity) Daniel + mistress = x = 2)

= 4(2) + 4(2), or 2 Dear Deidre questions of 8 paragraphs each.

2. Cherry

* Dating a married man (x = 2)
* Thinking of moving another country to be with a married man (x = 2)
* Cheating emotionally on her lover with Ben (x = 3)
* Cheating emotionally with another girl's boyfriend (x = 3)
* Isn't sure who she loves (x = 1)

= 4(2) + 4(2) + 4(3) + 4(3) + 4(1), or 5 Dear Deidre questions for a total of 44 paragraphs.

3. Ben

* Chasing after a woman who probably won't end up with him
* Chasing after a woman who is dating a married man
* Emotionally cheating on his girlfriend
* Can't figure out if he loves his girlfriend

= 4 questions, 32 paragraphs total.

4. Alice

* Dating a man who doesn't know if he loves her
* Trying to figure out if she should forgive her boyfriend for emotionally (and possibly physically?) cheating on her
* Dealing with a boyfriend who let others know about a pregnancy scare
* Trying to re-establish trust in a relationship if she sticks with Ben OR trying to figure out how to pick up the pieces after he dumps her for Cherry

= *4 questions, 40 paragraphs!*

I think it's fair to say everyone involved will have severe hand cramps at the very least.

Now, there is some room for interpretation here depending on how you divide the questions, but that comes to a total of approximately FIFTEEN possibilities for agony aunt questions, and none of them very short letters either, or in other words an entire Dear Deidre mailbag. And *each* of those questions has a simple answer:

Pack your bag and get out already, Alice! These people are crazy! Do you want to be crazy too? No? Then run!

What do you reckon your letter-writing threshold would be? Mine is, at most, one. I know that's harsh, but it is better to know your limits than to be emotionally bulldozed because you didn't respect them. Your tolerance may be higher. But fifteen? That's opera-level madness! That's Lucrezia Borgia-level! Sure, she inspired some wicked art, but only after she *died in child-birth*.

So here is the real question: is Alice a glutton for punishment? Are you? Do you want to be in a relationship that has enough drama in it to take you to February 2029? Is it worth it? Or would it be better to extricate yourself from this nonsense and find a good man who does not encourage others to attach their emotional baggage to him and who actually loves you?

Ending a relationship: the canonical step-by-step guide to the best breakup he'll ever have

Most of my close male friends are people I have slept with and even had significant romantic relationships with. The fact that we are on speaking terms at all probably says more about them than it does about me. But if you do want to keep your exes as friends — and even if you don't, but prefer not to be a complete bitch in a breakup — there is a very specific skill you must learn: how to let someone down easy, but firmly.

One thing that never suits is using a breakup to cram in even more criticism and hurt than strictly necessary. And yet, people seem to use the event to do just that. Be sensible: he is already going to be bereft of your pleasurable company, so you already know he will be hurt. Why add to that? It would be the very definition of cruelty.

However, take too subtle and circuitous an approach, and you might end up with what you thought was going to be a split only to find it isn't at all, because he hasn't got the point. You need to get the job done, but in a way befitting a lady such as yourself.

It sounds like a straightforward job, and in fact it is. However, it also seems to be something that some people simply can't learn how to do even after repeated breakups. They end up insulting the dumpee, or getting back together out of a fear of being alone, or just disappearing off the face of the earth rather than stand up and do the honourable thing. If a man was ending it with you, you would expect at least some kindness and honesty, right? Exactly. Be the dumper you would want to be dumped by.

Aged only eighteen I was on the receiving end of a one-sided breakup that could have turned into drama and heartbreak. After all, we were both teenagers, we had got together at a difficult time in his life, and naturally I thought the bond was strong and everlasting. On paper the end of the relationship should have been the worst thing to ever happen to me up to that point. And while the experience was disappointing and sad, it actually became a window of insight into how adults deal with difficult choices. To this day it is still the best breakup I ever had. You can do it too: it is a technique appropriate for all types of woman and can be broken down into four easy-to-remember steps:

1. Set the scene carefully.

He suggested we meet on neutral ground. This is an important point, don't ignore it. Don't have him round to your house, don't go over to his. Make it somewhere average and forgettable: a greasy spoon or a coffee place will do. A park, but don't bring a picnic. A bus shelter. You get the picture.

2. Timing is everything.

Don't do it when you've gone off somewhere exotic together. I say this from experience: it is important that the breakup doesn't come on the Monday of a one-week holiday. Or indeed anywhere in a shared holiday at all. After delivering 'the chat', you will need to get away, and also afford the Man his own space to think. If you do it when you still have time together anything could happen; if you wait until the end, you will be agonising over it the whole time.

3. Have a script and stick to it.

He had clearly thought through what he wanted to say and delivered it with utter conviction. No *maybe*, no *if*. A decision was made. It was a nonjudgemental one. The man handled it masterfully and should give lessons in how to do it. The structure of 'the chat' followed these points:

* There is nothing wrong with you. We get along really well. You are smart, attractive, fun, &c. (list of positive qualities).
* But I'm not feeling strongly about this, and it's important to me to feel passionate about relationships in general.

* You deserve someone who is passionate about being with you. It is unfortunate but I can't be that person.
* I don't want to prevent you having the amazing life you will soon be having with someone who is ready for you, so it's best we split now so you are free and clear.
* I struggled with this because you're nice and I don't want to hurt you. I didn't make the decision lightly but am sure it's the right thing.
* Do you have anything to ask me?

4. Get out of there.

Self-explanatory, I think.

Well I for one was blown away. He didn't want me... but! I actually felt good about this! Not my fault! I was great – better than great, I was wonderful! Just not right for *him*. A tiny detail, really, in the grand scheme of things. Plenty of fish and all that.

If you spotted that this was the old 'it's not you, it's me' line but with loads of cushioning, you are correct. The trick seems to be in making it crystal clear that the decision isn't negotiable and you're not wishy-washy about it, but also make it clear that there's nothing wrong with him and there's a lot of really great stuff about him. So it's more 'it's not you, it's not me, it's just not a fit, and I was able to see that more clearly after some time to think about us.' Oh, and leave promptly afterwards, before you're tempted to have breakup sex.

Being turned down: letting go lightly

In much the same way that we have our own warning signs regarding making it through the shallow shoals of relationship breakups, so do men. Only they're crap at it. They extend phase 1 — in which it is okay simply to disappear — for as long as possible, in some cases to the point where he leaves you with four screaming kids, saying he's going out for milk and never comes home. But that is the exception as far as I know. Most men consider anything up to after date three to be prime time to pull the disappearing act. So if he's done that, accept it and move on. With any luck you'll have a considerable number of men on backup duty so that you can still dig up a date for the weekend and not feel too bad about it. If not, pour the bath, pop some Tom Waits on the stereo, and scream at the walls about what a colossal jerkface he is. Then ring someone else and make a date for Friday night. Don't question it. Just do it.

As the relationship progresses, however, it slowly starts to dawn on a man that the fuck-and-ditch approach is perhaps not a good way forward, and that the woman in his life might appreciate something approximating a conversation in the leadup to a relationship breakdown. This all sounds well and good, until he starts considering the possibilities:

* You might set his belongings on fire.
* You might blog about him.
* You might find, and boil, his small furry pets.
* You might take the opportunity to tell him he has a

small penis/you screwed his brother/his breath smells.

None of which, I hope it does not need saying, are ideal results or what he wants to experience during what is already a stressful situation. And believe it or not, in spite of how you might feel in the heat of the moment, it isn't actually in your best interest either.

Yes, you might burn off some frustration in the short term by letting your inner id go wild. And who can say that at that moment it isn't a little bit fun to be cruelly and brutally honest. But the end result is that you probably look like a twat. An unattractive twat. An unattractive twat with about as much chance of retaining any sense of self-esteem when she looks back on the episode as a cat has of not licking its arse (in other words, none).

Whatever he says, regardless of your real reaction, you should be prepared. It will throw him off-kilter, and more to the point, you will come out of it looking like it was a decision made in your best interests, not his. Win-win.

So when he says:	You might be thinking:	You should say instead:
I'm not sure you have what I'm looking for in a partner.	You mean, breast implants and half a brain?	You're right, I think we have different expectations.
I'm too busy to be in a relationship right now.	...unless it's with porn...	You know, I'm pretty busy too. Good luck with things.

| You're a great girl but I just don't feel that spark with you. | Not the way you do when looking down your co-worker's cleavage, certainly. | That is a pity, but I understand completely what you're feeling. Bye. |
| I need someone who can offer me more support. | Which is why your mother still does your laundry, right? | That's too bad. I need someone more independent. Good luck. |

You might have already picked out a wedding dress and named your children, but the bottom line is when someone doesn't want you they don't want you and you can't make them any more than a man you've rejected could make you want him. So keep your dignity, if not your daydreams: smile, nod, agree with him and walk away. If he didn't want you, then clearly he isn't good enough for you anyway, right?

OMG! Not AGAIN!

...or, how not to date the same guy over. And over. And over.

Even once you've mastered the art of the breakup, it can be all too soon before you find yourself in the same situation — again. One the one hand, great: you get to practice splitting with unsuitable men until you have it down cold. But on the other hand, you're so clued up about relationships! You've learned so much! So why does it always happen that by month three of the relationship, he's borrowing money off you, the sex has tailed off to nearly zero, and he never does all the silly little romantic things that drew you in the first place, and you find yourself getting ready to have The Talk all over again *just like the last one?!?*

Or even worse, he splits with you – usually with the 'you're nice, but I'm just not feeling it anymore' line.

And to add insult to injury, you have this friend who seems to never struggle in relationships, who has quality men chasing after her all the time – or perhaps has selected one eligible bachelor from the rest, and is already hurtling rapidly towards commitment. And as far as you can see, she hasn't all that much going for her (or no more than you have, anyway)!

Is it a streak of rubbish men that just happens to have lasted since 1997? Is it bad luck? Are all men basically crap? Or... something else?

Does this seem familiar to you?

Dear Belle,

I am a woman in my mid 30s and have great relationships with my family and friends. It's relationships with men where I am having trouble.

Before you say I'm dating losers, you should know I'm actually very picky. These men are smart, funny, interesting, all have been employed and functional in society, but over time they turn out to be selfish and manipulative.

I tend to date people from my friend group so by the time we are involved there is already a good base of knowledge about each other, as well as mutual interests and mutual friends. In the beginning I feel valued and respected. They say I am easy to talk to, low-drama, funny, and always there when they need me.

I am not demanding. I have my own interests and don't need to be with someone 24/7. Having said that when I am involved I make myself available and love to spend time with just that person or out together doing things with friends.

So things seem great and I relax. And that's when every-thing starts to change. Suddenly if a day or two goes by with no contact and I call, this is deemed 'needy', even if in the early days he called me two or three times a day 'just to say hi' or because he was 'bored at work'.

Or if plans change or something comes up I'm totally cool with that, but eventually when we make plans he is late or does not show up at all, calling sometimes to cancel but more often than not just doesn't show.

And eventually they start asking to borrow money. They just turn out to be so different than who they were when we were just friends...

I don't know how to do it differently really but I'll take all the advice I can get. Thanks so much for your thoughts and input.

From,
  Average Reader

It doesn't matter whether you're a Plain Jane or a Good Girl, you're equally susceptible to dating the same man over and over. You can even be a Scary Bitch and fall into this trap — honey, I'm the canonical SB, and even I went through a thoroughly depressing spate in my 20s being taken for granted by a series of unsuitable men.

So I'm going to say something that may be hard to read, but is undoubtedly the truth. And I only know this because sister, I have been there. I could have written that very same letter. I have been the girl this always happened to.

How did I get over it? I had to learn five very important things, not only about relationships, but about myself.

Lesson 1: You don't keep dating the same guy... they keep dating the same girl.

I'll put it another way. If you don't want to date guys who borrow money and stand you up, don't be the kind of woman who puts up with those things. You repeatedly get stood up? What the fuck are you doing dating someone who stands you up? Stop giving men the impression that it's okay for them to stand you up. You do this by leaving them when they do it, not by asking when your next dinner date is.

Look in a mirror or a similar shiny object. That person staring back at you is the common denominator in all three instances.

Whether you admit it or not, you are choosing men based on their similar traits. Surprise — they're all reacting the same way, because you have chosen this type of person. It's as if the men you choose surprise you with their secret hatred of kittens, and you're not realising that you're getting your date list from the I Kick Cats Local 321.

Lesson 2: It's okay to want whatever you want.

Everyone has dealmakers and dealbreakers, and you should stick to whatever yours are without exception. Let's say your ideal list is something like this:

1.) You want a real boyfriend, not one who will only call you his 'friend' in public.
2.) You want someone who respects your time and doesn't stand you up.
3.) You want someone who won't take you for granted over time.

It's not crazy to want those things, or whatever your things are. So go looking for them. Be clear about them. Stop settling. And when someone does that stuff to you — the clingy accusation, the jealous pout, the standing you up — don't react by changing what you want just to keep the relationship going.

It's entirely fair to ask to be treated well. The type of men you're picking can't do it — that's why he's trying to fall into easy interactions where you're already friends — so stay away from this. Look for men who can. They're out there. You have to know what you want and stand up for it, though. And go after it.

Lesson 3: Don't date inside your friend group.

Consider a more proactive dating situation, rather than a reactive one. Sometimes relationships that 'just happen' are really about someone taking advantage of someone who seems easy to become intimate with, since you already know each other. The men haven't had to work all that hard to get with you, and you haven't been out there seeking someone whose values you share. You're right there, you're open to it, they have needs, so why not?

Contrary to what romantic comedies would have us believe, the gradual evolution into relationship scenario isn't actually a great start to a relationship. It's more of a default in which no one has to take responsibility for putting themselves out there as potential dating material. The bar is set too low.

In other words, it might be that you could do a lot better than these guys – but maybe that you aren't secure enough to reach out to the wider world of potential partners, maybe you're a little afraid of relationships, maybe you don't prioritise relationships highly, maybe you're pressed for time, so you don't end up pursuing the men who would be better. Instead you end up settling for men who are just... around a lot. And those tend to be the ones who have less to offer – because if they did, well, they would be out working on dating somebody fabulous too.

Lesson 4: Choose differently (but not too different).

You like bookish, nerdy intellectuals? Date a fire-fighter. Like 'em beefy and light on brain power? Consider taking less arm candy, more mind candy into your world. Mix it up. Don't discount anyone based on his CV alone, or because you don't usually date single dads/Brummies/gingers/whatever. Variety really and truly is the spice of life.

But at the same time, be sure not to use your last failed relationship as the anti-template for the next one. As appealing as, say, dating a Marine would be when your last horrible boyfriend was a G20 protester, exact opposite of the last guy as a criterion for successfully choosing a mate is fraught with problems. You'll always be comparing him to the last one. At some point he may realise it (probably because you slipped and told him), and resent you for it. And really, Exact Opposite as revenge has the distinct whiff of teenage rebellion about it — sort of like becoming an atheist solely because your parents forced parochial school on you, not because you actually buy into the logic.

Lesson 5: Take no shit.

Long ago and far away back in uni, I was part of a social group where the women strove to be 'low maintenance' because men talked about what a pain 'high maintenance girls' were. Being young, we went too far. In an effort to not be too much we were often spineless and took a lot of crap. The high maintenance girls got all the respect. We couldn't figure it out.

Things have equalised since; being too demanding and drama-filled is rubbish, but the lesson from that era of my life stands. These days, if I got the needy line for calling after two days, I would answer with 'this is not needy, this is what boyfriends and girlfriends do. If you think this is needy, you have some things to figure out. Call me when you get through with that.'

You don't want someone whose boundaries are so inconsistent that you're on the phone three times a day one week, being called 'clingy' the next. You want someone who knows they want to be in a relationship and knows they want it to be with you. You want someone who doesn't miss your dates and ignore your communications. You want someone mature.

If you don't stand up for yourself, most people lose respect for you. I really wish it wasn't the case – and there was a time when I would protest about how *unfair* it was, how people *shouldn't* be this way, how you should be able to be your fully caring, easygoing, giving self and expect the other person to give you the same. But that's just not how human nature works. If you don't draw the line, people will push it further and further. They don't even realise they're doing it, don't think of themselves as taking advantage of you, because they've got used to you as a person who is always there for their needs.

CHAPTER 8

Successfully Single

— being a SPINSTER

My mother, bless her, imparted exactly one useful piece of romantic advice to us girls: never trust a man in a V-neck jumper. Granted, that has at least prevented me from going down the Simon Cowell route, but as a comprehensive source of counsel she left much to be desired. If, like me, your mother was not exactly forthcoming with her successful hints and tips, here is a salient point to consider...

Relationships, Eh. Who Needs 'Em?

When I was young I thought that when people fell in love they'd have wondrous sex and be all happy and bluebirds would sing around their heads as they consummated their beautiful relationship in sunlit sheets and glorious passion. They'd live happily ever after as best friends with loads of hot backdoor action on a regular basis.

The reality...

Scenario 1: You meet someone, you have drunken sex; later you have sober sex, it's okay — nice even, and you have all those new relationship hormones buzzing around; you like them, you fall in love, the sex is okay; it tails off, you have a very loving but asexual relationship. Touching them feels wrong because you're so close to them it's practically incest, and not in a good way. You can't do sex but you can do love.

Scenario 2: You meet someone, you have drunken sex, it's dirty as fuck, it's hot sexy hot hot sexytime amazing sexy hot; later you have sober sex (though it's better drunk); your relationship is a train-wreck, you can't call it love, you don't know what's happening emotionally but you can't be in the same room as them without tearing off their clothes; you exhaust each other in a perpetual state of mutually assured destruction, but the sex is AWESOME. You can't do love but you can do sex.

In complete honesty scenario 2 is more fun, though perhaps less socially acceptable, than scenario 1 and therefore a better lifestyle option until Mr Right-and-Forever-Sexy comes along (if indeed he ever does). Disregard the rubbish you read about the new, liberated women post-whatever stupid television show is meant to represent the zeitgeist lately. It's all rubbish. There is far too much judgement and moral-ising about single women enjoying sex in the manner and as often as they like it — be that four times daily, or once a quarter.

These strange ideas that dominated my youth sprung from the dangerous and entirely false notion of the Soul Mate, as thrust upon us by:

* Media: celeb mags, personality profiles.
* Entertainment: novels, chick flicks, et al.
* Well-meaning elder female relatives.
* The entire fucking universe.

I do so hate to burst anyone's bubble here – okay, you are correct, I don't – but the very notion of one person in the world, ever, being the one you are 'meant', 'fated', or otherwise hippy-dippy mumbo jumbo joined-astrally-forever with is bollocks*, in my humble opinion. This can be disproven on simply statistical grounds: in the entire history of the human race, what are the odds that the perfect person will be the right age for you at the right time, and happen to be *exactly where you happen to be* at that moment?

Answer: slim to none, baby, and slim's on a diet.

What is far more likely to happen in my experience is that you meet someone – or several someones – over the course of your life whose qualities somewhat approximate your ideal lover, and whose company you can stand for 2+ years. I've been accused of being unnecessarily pessimistic on this point, but I'll make it

---

* (N.B.: True Fated Love may not actually be bollocks. Belle de Jour claims no responsibility for existence or otherwise of True Fated Love. No exchanges and no returns. Your statutory rights are not affected.)

again all the same: no one knows yourself like you do, no one ever can. You come into the world alone (bar the handful of offspring from overinseminated American would-be reality show queens). In your mind you live alone. When you die you will be alone. That is all.

Well, that cheery note aside, let's talk about being single!

A distinct problem with the single life is the assumption that single equals lonely. Sometimes, yes, that can be true – who hasn't sobbed into a pillow from time to time over the notion that The One might already have come and gone? Smug updates from happily paired friends can also be a source of stress and self-doubt. But in both of these instances, it is important to remember:

* Your friends are only presenting the public face – i.e. the most positive aspects – of their relationship.
* No matter what they say about the sex staying hot, they still have to watch him floss and he probably farts loads, too.
* Being in a couple is no inoculation against loneliness – you've felt just as lonely with a boyfriend before, remember?
* Feelings are fleeting things. Sometimes I also feel like I might want to wake up tomorrow morning as a kitten, but it passes.

Still, it can be close to impossible to keep such things in perspective when everyone from your mum to that irritating girl from your school you inadvertently recontacted on the internet and now can't seem to shake, are so unflinchingly convinced that life as one half of a pair is inherently better than life as a single, regardless of circumstances.

Um, no.

Which is why I am calling for a new initiative: the SPINSTER movement.

Why spinster? Because it is time to finally reclaim a horrific and vitriolic accusation from the lips of the abusers. Because it spells out some really nifty acronyms when expanded. Because it ever-so-slightly invoked the image of an army of single women dressed like spiders. In short, because it's cool.

QUESTION 1: *So what does SPINSTER stand for?*

<u>S</u>he
<u>P</u>refers
<u>I</u>ndependent
<u>N</u>o-strings
<u>S</u>ex
<u>T</u>o
<u>E</u>ntering
<u>R</u>elationships

(or perhaps, *Entering Regrettable Relationships*. But SPIN-STERR would just look odd.)

Though perhaps no-strings sex isn't your thing. In which case, feel free to substitute any appropriate hobby or interest that fits, such as:

* Nightly Stockbrokerage
* Nappy Sewing
* Nun Stalking
* Narwhal Sighting
* ...and so on.

At the first meeting of the local SPINSTER union, we discussed the benefits of single living:

1.) You can come home pissed.
2.) You can come home pissed whenever you like.
3.) You can come home pissed whenever you like, and fall asleep in your clothes.
4.) You can come home pissed whenever you like, and fall asleep in your clothes on the bathroom floor.

Truly, this is what the modern world was meant for. In addition to the list we managed to compile over a bottle or three of Nero d'Avola, these other benefits come to mind:

5.) Your lady-razor will not mysteriously relocate from the shower to the sink with a telltale residue of black stubble dried into the blade.
6.) There are never any arguments about whose turn it is to do the washing up.
7.) The radio is always tuned to the station where you left it.
8.) You can listen to whatever crap music you like, at whatever hour you prefer, at a volume which exactly pleases you, for the duration you prefer.

It probably goes without saying that the benefits are actually innumerable, and have much to do with not having to compromise your living style and domestic preferences. Someone else finishing the milk and forgetting to replace it is non-existent. Comments re: your predilection for picking up chips on the way home from work goes uncommented.

In short, like Burger King, you get it Your Way. And that is exactly what our feminine forebears threw themselves in front of horses for. It would be rude not to revel in the success of their struggle.

QUESTION 2: *How do you know you qualify as a SPINSTER?*

The signs are subtle and can accumulate without your ever noticing, but after a point people stop introducing you to this 'amazing friend of my boyfriend... you'll love him' and default to buying you slipper socks at Christmas. Far from being the end of the world, this is, in fact, the very beginning of a new phase in your life: the much discussed, yet rarely actually achieved, Not Giving a Toss What Other People Think. Here are some other signs that freedom is soon to be yours:

* Your family have stopped issuing +1 invites to weddings and holidays.
* Your mother has stopped tearing up whenever the word 'granny' is mentioned.
* Your Facebook relationship status is permanently set to 'It's complicated'.

* Calling a man your 'friend' automatically implies you have probably slept with him.
* Your options to hand for birth control number at least two and possibly as many as four.
* You genuinely do not care how you're going to meet the next one.

What a SPINSTER understands, and the rest of the world seems awfully keen to forget, is that other relationships are worth nurturing just as much as romantic ones. Friends and lovers – you need plenty of both. And just as with the friends who move through your life, sometimes for only a few weeks but touch you with their kindness and joy nonetheless, it's okay to see someone for only a short time and move on with nary a word breathed about commitment.

QUESTION 3: *What are the requirements of successful SPINSTER living?*

Oh, there are many. Your top ten will depend on your type – whether a GG, PJ or SB, the details can vary. What a lot of SPINSTERs have in common though is:

* Being supportive of other women regardless of relationship status.
* Not letting the bastards get you down.
* Having a busy, active life.
* Being independent both emotionally and financially.
* Being honest.

Now let's consider each of these in more detail.

1. Being supportive of other women regardless of relationship status

It is generally observed that women are the harshest critics of other women. Whether it is because of how they dress, how they act or the details of their private lives, women can be counted on to be the most vocal and hateful of judges. And yet, it doesn't have to be that way — in fact it shouldn't. Not just on the general, *heat*-readership level, but towards the women in your daily life as well.

Do you silently judge your co-worker's wardrobe, or raise a discreet eyebrow at your friend's choice of food, not to mention boyfriend? Fucking stop that. It helps no one, least of all your own self-esteem — because if you are quietly judging others, you will become paranoid that they are judging you, too. So when it comes to the women in your life, be a good friend when they're heartbroken and be genuinely happy when they find someone great.

On a side note, generally speaking when we are critical of each other it is because we're projecting our own insecurities onto them. So the next time you find yourself doing that, why not stop and think a moment about how you are judging yourself, as well? Turn the words back around, this time directed at yourself. Does it seem harsh? Unfair? Would you be angry if someone said the same thing back to you? Food for thought…

If you're a GG, this means stepping up perhaps more than you might usually do. Be the friend who suggests a night out, or quiet drinks down the pub. Or even a night in with a DVD. Don't be tempted to fade into the background, friendship-wise, be the rock.

If you're a PJ, this means being available for a chat and being a great listener. People genuinely appreciate someone who can listen, and those qualities are in short supply. So now is the time to hone your empathetic ear; and don't tune out. What you learn about yourself, your own prefer-ences and ways in which others' lessons can be applied to your own life, is invaluable.

If you're a SB, this means bringing a bottle of hard spirits round when good news breaks. As well as bad.

2. Not letting the bastards get you down

Unfortunately, this is a fact of life that cannot be changed: people are nosy and tactless. Don't give me that — you know it's true. You are as well. It is far more fitting to the modern SPINSTER to learn how to handle such exchanges, rather than wishing them away, 'cos the odds of that happening are about as likely as me claiming born-again virginity.

From time to time, some well-meaning idiot will ask when you're going to settle down. Don't take this as a cue to run crying to the toilets or to go off on a rant. You're far too good for that.

If you're a GG, this means smiling politely and quickly finding somewhere else to be (or if physical relocation is not an option, changing the subject). Happily, with your well-honed skills of Faking It Until You Make It, you're a natural at this. Score one for yourself and move on.

If you're a PJ, this means letting them have their say, then logically – and politely – informing them that you are perfectly happy in your life as it is. Then possibly undercutting their situation with a well-placed remark, preferably in front of their other half. 'Oh, I know – I'm just ever so selective about men. Which reminds me, I ran into several of your exes last week...'

If you're a SB, this means learning how to physically restrain yourself from rolling your eyes/beheading your opponent/laying waste to any and all couples within a five-mile radius. You're strong; you can handle this, and probably without attracting the attention of the local constabulary as well.

3. Having a busy, active life

Have loads to do. Meet people. Engage in interesting, fun activities. Love your work. Don't make a man-shaped hole in your life then waste time looking at it longingly. Dear me, it sounds so easy, but this is the one most people struggle with, especially when striking out into something new on your tod. Motivation is a factor – it's easier to go along to something if you know someone is going with you. But also there is the deeply ingrained need for approval, and turning up some-where alone feels like failure. Everyone is staring, judging. Safety in numbers and all that.

Um, earth to Narcissus! No one worth caring about gives a monkey's how many people you walk around in public with. If you are incapable of using the toilet without a squadron supporting your every step, now is the time to break the habit. Go to the cinema... turn up for an activity... eat a meal out... alone. Go on holiday solo. If you have ever in your heart of hearts wondered whether you got into or stayed in a relationship simply because you cannot bear solitude (or worse still, been accused of same) then this is of particular importance.

Mastering the art of being busy and independently active means never wondering whether your motivations for choosing a man were entirely kosher again. Poet Gregory Corso wrote that standing on a street corner waiting for no one is power, and it is absolutely, without question the truth.

> *If you're a GG*, this means encouraging your natural talents and interests. If you're the crafty sort, there are all manner of groups to join and classes to take. And helpfully, having something else to focus on means you can interact with the others around you exactly as much as you're comfortable with, without seeming odd for drifting off into your own little world.

> *If you're a PJ*, this means getting out and about. Maybe you thought your pubbing and clubbing days ended with the third year of uni, or that those

sort of entertainments don't satisfy you anymore. Bollocks. Fun is fun at whatever age. In fact, it can be fun to regress even more: take up residence on the swings in the park, rediscover skipping ropes. Play.

If you're a SB, this means doing what you do naturally. What, you want me to tell the social butterflies of the world how to suck eggs? Fuhgeddaboudit.

4. Being independent both emotionally and financially

There is a stereotype that refuses to die – the gold-digger stereotype. Now while the imagery that goes with the phrase is laughable (the Gucci, the bling, the five-inch-heels, the Tango tan) the reality is far more pervasive and far more subtle. Hoping to go down to half-time once you start a family? Um... who is financing that? Think you should have equal equity on any future houses even if your husband earns significantly more? Again, consider the implications re: *relationship* equity. Silently grouse over the fact that the flowers you were sent last Valentine's were somewhat smaller than the opulent display delivered to the office next door? Now, don't make me say it...

In short, the condition of femininity is insufficient reason to expect other people to provide for you. If someone offers assistance, be certain to accept it gracefully. But don't treat it as your due. It is nice to feel lovely and adored. It is less nice to give the impression that you are ungrateful when people do so.

Emotional independence works on a similar level. None of this 'you complete me' shite — how scary is that? Many women seem to think it perfectly acceptable to postpone their own happiness until the moment Prince Charming arrives on the scene (and then are flummoxed when he looks round, surveys the possibilities, and fucks off to parts unknown). Well, durrrr. Would you be attracted to a man who held your hands, looked soulfully into your eyes, and sincerely intoned that meeting you had been the happiness he had always dreamed of? Fuck no. That's a one-way ticket to Stalkerville.

If you're a GG, this means pushing harder to go for the job you always wanted. You had a dream once, remember? So maybe being a Princess Astronaut is stretching the boundaries of plausibility some- what — but at least one of those goals might just be achievable with hard work and dedication. Make an oath to push your limits and surprise yourself.

If you're a PJ, this means stop asking Daddy for money. Go out on dates. Stop telling guys you love them on the third date, and no, being drunk is *not* a good enough excuse.

If you're a SB, this means... hell, if you're not already running a FTSE company and finding inner peace I don't really know why you're reading this paragraph. Take the quiz again and come back when you've been resorted into GG or PJ.

5. Being honest

We've already discussed men and honesty — now let us peer at the other side of the coin. Both sexes are frequently guilty of misrepresentation, albeit often for different ends...

One thing a lot of women have grown very good at is suppressing their feelings in order to please other people. Not only is this harmful, it's irritating. You might think you are calm, unruffled and in control, when in all honesty you're probably coming across as uptight and insincere. (Where do I get off saying that, right? Hey, I never said I was going to be nice about this. Not to mention: I myself have often been accused of being uptight and insincere, so I know of what I speak here.)

So it is essential to be as honest as you can be. But not, you know, to the point at which it's offensive. There is such a thing as compulsive truth-telling, and it's a little like emotional Tourette's. No, not that. More like having the courage to acknowledge your own feelings and let people in on what you are thinking in a reasonable manner.

Example: someone has just made you angry. Let's say your sister has stood you up. Pushing it down goes a little like: 'No problem, this does not bother me, continue as normal.' In other words, Continue to Walk All Over Me. Emotional Tourette's responds: 'I knew it, you always disappoint me, you always do things like this!' In other words, I Will Exaggerate Facts to the Point at Which I Make No Sense.

Can you see how the first approach is clearly dishonest, and the second is blaming someone's personality for what was really a one-off action?

There is, happily, a third way: 'When you did that, I felt taken advantage of. Don't do it again.' In other words, identify honestly what you are feeling – and set a spoken limit on the behaviour you expect from others – but don't say everything about her is bad and wrong. Being known as someone whose opinion is always considered and not fake – that is the mark of an excellent SPINSTER.

> *If you're a GG*, this means speaking up for yourself every now and again. While no one likes to spoil the mood, it is important to remember that a little too much self-containment can actually be read as misleading, which is the last thing you want.

> *If you're a PJ*, this means not stuffing down your real feelings until they inevitably explode – most likely at a family get-together, in front of someone you're on a second date with, or sobbing in his arms right after the first time you have sex. Let the pressure cooker let off a little steam from time to time, and avoid the giant bust-ups. You'll feel ever so much better.

> *If you're a SB*, this means sometimes swapping what you could say strictly to get ahead for what you could say to underline your trustworthiness. Men – and people in general – want to feel their

emotions are safe with you. By giving a little in the way of vulnerability and honest connection, you will be amply rewarded in kind. Then you can screw the bastards later.

To recap...

You don't need to be single to be a Spinster, but understanding the Tao of Spinster often comes from periods of singlehood. If you find yourself in just such a situation now, congratulations! You are embarking on an exciting journey to learning about yourself. Don't give it up for just anyone. And if you do happen to settle down, remember you can do so whilst still retaining important elements of independence — as well as being sympathetic to other women on the Spinster path.

Remember the war cry of the Spinster is independence: romantic, intellectual, financial, sartorial. Challenging the status quo not by shouting and protesting too much, but by being an authentic person following her authentic desires, wherever that might take her.

CHAPTER 9

A Cautionary Interlude

— sex work

Why you aren't hooker material

Digging through the email inbox archives, I find a lot of letters similar to this:

Dear Belle,

I wanted to say how much I admire you!! I'm single and have recently been approached by a married man who wants to pay to have sex with me. What should I tell him? How much should I charge?

Or this:

Dear Belle,

I love your books!! As a recent graduate I've been having trouble finding a job and was wondering which agency you worked for? I really need the cash!

Or this:

Dear Belle,

I love sex!! Can I make some money on the side? Tell me where to meet men who will pay for it!

What do all these letters have in common? (Apart from their good taste in reading material of course.) It is that by and large, without having considered the practicalities of sex work, the writers are seeking advice (and not a small amount of hand-holding).

Call me a harsh bitch — you wouldn't be the first — but I tend to think if someone has done not even a basic amount of research, I am not obliged to help them out in any way. Since when was I the JobCentre for hookers? Still, because sex work is controversial — and because there can be some risks involved — I do tend to reply. If only to discourage them.

But... discourage? What ever for? Is it because I can't stand the competition? Or maybe that I'm naturally mean spirited? *Au contraire*. It is because, by and large, 99% of the women I have ever met in my life would make terrible sex workers, and odds are these question-askers fall squarely into that category.

You see, if one desires to be successful at sex work, you must accept that at heart it is not a glamorous lifestyle, but rather a customer service position.

That is correct — I said customer service position. Sex work is about the clients, not the provider. What they get out of it, not what the girls get out of it. And that is why it is a non-starter for most people as a career and best avoided. It is not for your common-or-garden shagger. It does not suit girls with a one-track mind. It is not a self-fulfilment odyssey. If what you seek is adventure, go on holiday. If it's orgasms, cultivate a sensitive lover. But if you imagine either of those is the predetermined outcome of a call girl career, then oh honey, you could not be more wrong. Here is how to spot the difference between someone who does it for pleasure, and someone who does it for a job:

The Common-or-Garden Shagger... goes out with a short skirt, her key and some cash in a tiny clutch bag.

The Call Girl... goes out with a bag that could double as a floatation device, if it wasn't crammed to the gills with condoms and vibrators.

The Common-or-Garden Shagger... wears whatever she fancies.

The Call Girl... wears what she thinks the client will fancy.

The Common-or-Garden Shagger... rings when she arrives home, so her friends know she is safe.

The Call Girl... rings when she arrives at the appointment, so her manager doesn't have to go chasing her down.

The Common-or-Garden Shagger... has half a bottle of wine before a big night.

The Call Girl... has a pore-tightening facial and an excruciating pubic plucking before a big night.

The Common-or-Garden Shagger... stays in if she isn't feeling up to going out, and sleeps alone if she isn't up to having sex.

The Call Girl... is always available (or gives the appear-ance of), and never has a headache.

The Common-or-Garden Shagger... loves telling her friends all about her exciting Friday night, down to the gory details.

The Call Girl... makes up excuses not to join her friends on Friday night. And the details will never pass her lips.

Sex work still sound like jolly fun? It is not for the faint of heart, nor for the easily bored. The hours are odd, the people are strange, and you are probably working for someone you hate. It's not unlike being employed to sit at the checkout at Asda, only with better uniforms and (slightly) more contact with the unwashed public.

Here are more than a few myths you might have had about being a call girl, busted...

The myth	*The reality*
Only rich and famous men use call girls, so a great tip is all but guaranteed. And I'll get to meet interesting people!	Loads of men use call girls – not just the rich. (Who are often dull to a fault.) And they are the stingiest with their tips as well.
Preparation? What prepara-tion? I'm well fit! Just pop on a nice frock and party makeup, and I'm set to go.	The client is judging you from the moment he opens the door – and you probably fall somewhat short of his expect-ations. Even if you look your best he may not like it.

I'm a night person anyway! This job suits my preferred hours, and I can have the mornings to myself.	Ever heard of the lunchtime rush? Or been prepared to go out completely sober and looking box-fresh at 4 a.m.? The world does not revolve around your sleep schedule.
Even handsome men use sex workers, so I can just sit back and pick and choose the ones I fancy.	For every prince, you have to kiss at least ten toads. And there is usually a good reason why the princes are seeing call girls…
It's only having sex, why bother being organised?	Tell that to the manager when you've 'forgotten' to deposit her cut in the bank… again.
I can just close the door and let it go. Having sex with strangers does not trouble me.	If you ever – and I mean EVER – have had second thoughts about a one-night stand, or tried to change a fuck buddy into a boyfriend, THIS JOB IS NOT FOR YOU.

And regarding orgasms at work? I don't. They're paying for their orgasm, not mine. And letting go to the point of orgasm can be in direct conflict with keeping half an eye on the time… which is what they are technically paying me for, yeah?

However. Luckily for you, there is a silver lining:

vicarious experience. I went out and fucked men for money so you don't have to.

If nothing else, I like to think in many ways I was a good* call girl. And it was definitely a vocation in which the skilled practitioners were both born *and* made.

In order to be a better hooker, I needed decidedly more:

* Blowjob skills
* Sense of humour
* Sets of matching underwear

than I already had, coupled with significantly less:

* Body hair
* Using the arrival of my period as an all-purpose excuse
* Intolerance for people I wouldn't ordinarily fuck

than I originally possessed.

* Keep in mind that 'good' in this instance is neither indication of the content of one's character, nor the pureness of one's heart. 'Good' refers to success at handling the business end, that is to say, attracting clients and extracting money from them. Julia Roberts's character in *Pretty Woman* may have been a good person, but she was not a good hooker, because in a fit of... I don't know, stupidity, I think, or possibly Idiotic Screenwriters Twistmaking, certainly not conscience nor self preservation... she gave back the money in the end, remember? Not to mention she was charging far too little to act as what was essentially an executive companion (and what's more, Richard Gere, the sharkish businessman, would obviously have known that. Some white knight, eh, ladies? Care to marry him now? I bet he deducted from her fee for the condoms, too).

But it wasn't just about the depilation, oh no. There is a lot I learned, both about relationships with lovers and relationships in general, from being a call girl. So maybe someone else can benefit from the knowledge without having to go on the game. I present the main things I learned which may just benefit you:

1. Oral sex skills

No, it isn't necessarily the most nuanced item in the sexual bag of tricks, but for sheer bang-for-buck (sorry, couldn't resist) the good old blowjob cannot be beaten. In a world where double anal fisting is now passé even among suburban grannies, this will always have a place in your sexual repertoire. Always.

As regards oral technique, there is no shortage of guidance on this subject to be found everywhere from shiny women's magazines to internet fora. However, as we discussed before, there are two main points: saliva and enthusiasm. Whether you trace out the letters of the alphabet with the tip of your tongue on his glans or make like a Dyson and lose no suction is by the by. Just be certain things are well lubed, that you are (or are making a decent approximation of) enjoying it, and the rest should take care of itself.

Also: time expectations. If coming in your mouth is the goal, be aware of this. Many women appear to have calibrated their expectations of time between oral contact and ejaculation on sixteen-year-old boys, and I can assure you, that twenty-second record you are so proud of will not buy you much credibility among the fiftyish-and-Viagra set. Start slowly or risk lockjaw.

N.B. Any man who tries to impress you using the same technique is: a keeper. Marry him. Or at the least keep his number for emergencies.

2. Sense of humour

This, on the other hand, is the one thing call girls – and real-life girls – need above all else. You can give a shitty blowie, have client after client go soft on you, but a winning smile and a thick skin will see you through every time. There is something to be said for being able to face human men in all their glory with neither surprise nor disgust.

Embarrassing moments happen to everyone, it is a fact of life. While on the one hand there is a certain type of woman who will always set her alarm an hour earlier than her husband so she can get up, apply makeup, and go back to bed, that is neither a healthy nor realistic way to live.

Even if it's only for a hour, and you're being paid to be the perfect girlfriend, you will fanny fart. Fact. For the Alarm Clock Makeup brigade, this would probably be followed by extreme embarrassment, hiding in a closet, and twelve sessions with a therapist. So what should a well-adjusted woman do? Laugh, do a couple of squeezes to make certain the pelvic floor is in place, and get back to it. If he remembers it at all later, it won't be the most outstanding part of the evening.

N.B. Any man who tries to impress you using the same technique is: definite friendship material.

3. Matching underwear

The *sine qua non* of sexy grooming. It doesn't matter how expensive the constituent parts are, if they don't match, it will look like you dressed in the dark. While you might think this is acceptable in a Real Relationship, it will absolutely positively NOT lead to repeat business in the professional sphere. Which leads me to believe that most men would like to see sexy frillies on their girlfriends, not just hookers and hos. So as tempting as cute panties might be... invest only if there is a matching bra (or you plan to go commando on the upper half).

N.B. Any man who tries to impress you using the same technique is: since men can't really have matching underwear, not applicable. Clean is a good start though.

4. Body hair

I'm not here to tell you about the Brazilian or the Hollywood. You already know about the various topiaries available these days. I'm here to tell you that whatever arrangement you choose, from full bush to bald eagle, don't get caught halfsies. Shaving is only impressive if there is no stubble. If *au naturel* is to be your calling card, trimmed and combed is best (especially from the man giving oral sex point of view). Treat it as you would the hair on your head — style is up to personal preference, but whatever you do, keep it neat.

N.B. Any man who tries to impress you using the same technique is: probably a porn star, or the sort of person who will surreptitiously try to make a video of the two of you in the act. You are warned.

5. *Period days*

Ah, the sponge trick. There are days I wish I'd never written about that — having to answer questions about whether synthetic vs. natural sponges are healthier or work better is one thing, being accused of turning back feminism by twenty years merely for suggesting it might not be the worst thing in the world to have sex while the painters are in is another.

I mean, are there people in the world for whom sex stops one week of every month just because of the natural rhythm of their cycle? Really?

If you are one of these, well, go ahead and skip this tip.

Anyway, the sponge thing. I've used synthetic sponges but I am not a doctor and really, if you're taking feminine hygiene advice from a whore before running the idea past a licensed medical professional there are far bigger questions about your life that need to be addressed first. As in, now. But yeah, the sponge, it works for me. A comprehensive wash past the second day of my period works too. But if it's Red Sea time and there is absolutely no way you could possibly get jiggy without the hotel room looking like pigs were slaughtered there, well, I suppose you can always invent a death in the family.

N.B. Any man who tries to impress you using the same technique is: umm, a woman. Men don't do the bleed thing, remember?

6. Keeping your wits about you

Or to put it another way, maximising your skills at losing the (potentially dangerous) losers.

Here's a simple place to start: forget about the 'liquid courage' idea and don't drink loads before a date, and if there is drink on offer, don't get lashed. While I don't buy into the notion that women (and sex workers) are only moments away from rape and murder at all times, it is still a good idea to be as in control of a situation as you possibly can be. There are crazy men in the world. They do like to hurt people. Most of the people you meet in life for the first time will NOT be like that. But it doesn't hurt to keep an eye peeled for warning signs.

One clue when I was working: if someone keeps changing the time and location of the appointment, it is not a good sign. If there is no way to verify his real identity or phone number, ditto. If someone got short or angry with me because of this then I would definitely back off — someone who puts his whims before your reasonable safety requests will not be a good client.

Bottom line, I never put up with for money anything I wouldn't do for free.

Same with men in the free-date world. If he seems cagey, there could be good reasons for that. If you get it wrong, so what? There will be more men and more dates. And if you ignore what turns out to have been a genuine warning sign... well.

Cultivate an air of selectivity; it will attract better men to you and help keep you safer.

N.B. Any man who tries to impress you using the same technique is: a paranoid jerk.

7. Being less intolerant

...is not the same as being tolerant. It's about taking your inbuilt prejudice against the ugly/Conservative voters/whatever and dialling it down a notch. Or twelve.

I am often surprised how rude people can be to absolute strangers, people whose paths they will cross for twelve seconds and likely never see again (bus drivers of London, I am looking in *your* direction). If you are likely to fly off the handle simply because a chance interaction that meant little or nothing in the overall scheme of your daily life did not go precisely as you might have wished it, then maybe you shouldn't be interacting with other humans, hey? Much less going on dates.

If, on the other hand, you are particularly talented at jollying people along, then success with men is yours for the taking.

But wait – I hear you cry – how does this square with street smarts, and the need not to be a Pollyanna? Isn't being nice to people the very same quality that will get you into trouble?

Oh no, my dear. What will get you into trouble is being naïve and too trusting. But it is still possible to have a healthy sense of boundaries and a good eye for when a situation is turning to your disadvantage, and still be polite.

This is a concept I call the Velvet Hammer approach. The Velvet Hammer is a woman who manages to get exactly what she needs without causing offence, and in doing so, can often defuse a situation that would have escalated badly in lesser hands. There are particular qualities that distinguish a Velvet Hammer in action:

* Never raises her voice, unless calling for urgent help. When things are not going her way, she speaks more slowly, more clearly, and frequently, more sweetly.

* Does not give in to the urge to make cheap shots, throw insults, or bring up anything irrelevant to the task or discussion at hand. A Velvet Hammer stays focused and trusts the man will follow her lead.

* Does not let herself get distracted by his long-winded explanations or excuses. Velvet Hammers cut to the quick of the situation and are not fooled by an expensive bottle of champers and lies.

* Extracts herself from a situation — as politely as humanly possible — if it turns dangerous. And it goes without saying, a Velvet Hammer always has backup, be it a driver waiting around the corner, or an agent or friend on the other end of the telephone. She does not put herself out without protection.

* Beautiful manners are the calling card of the Velvet Hammer. She is skilled at turning men down in

such a way that they often don't realise that is what happened.

* Never trash-talks after the fact. If someone is unpleasant or dangerous, she reports this to the concerned parties in a factual way, then moves on. Nothing sticks to the Velvet Hammer.
* Treats her manager, colleagues, and clients with equal reasonability and consideration.

N.B. Any man who tries to impress you using the same technique is: a fucking saint.

8. Intimate familiarity with the Kama Sutra

Worry not, this does not involve mastery of the famed sixty-four positions of the document — unless you're an SB who already worked through those by the end of orientation week at uni. In fact, knowledge of the Kama Sutra can be (and often is) faked. Merely saying the words and then something vaguely authoritative — 'Kama being the Hindu god of love, of course, who like Cupid has a predilection for shooting people with arrows' — should be enough to hook someone into interested conversation with you.

N.B. Any man who tries to impress you using the same technique is: an arse and should be used for his money, then left. In other words, the perfect client.

9. A working knowledge of the past and current stars of pornography

Hands down, the single most impressive topic of conversation a woman can whip out at a party.

For most of their lives men have imagined the delights of visual stimulation via the media of film loop, sticky pages or ancient video to be strictly their terrain. And unlike when a woman starts in on her knowledge of pulling transmissions – sacrilege! – this is one area where they are willing, nay eager, to share.

And oh what an effective strategy you will find this to be when engaged in the art of clothed or unclothed stimulation. Simply by dropping the names Linda Lovelace, Rocco Sifreddi, and Ron Jeremy, you will have the boys eating out of your hand. Or you eating out of their laps. Whatever.

N.B. Any man who tries to impress you using the same technique is: someone who needs to get out more, with real ladies, who are preferably not you.

10. A healthy appreciation for gay culture

Face it, if you want to have frank and open discussions about things ranging from hair removal to penis size, it won't be with your straight girlfriends (those cracks about their man's endowment? They're lying). It definitely won't be with straight men, duh. And it most often won't be with other girls on the game – we're petrified by the thought of the competition gaining an edge.

No, if you want to talk shop, it's with the boys who like boys. So if in search of good, down-to-earth chat about mid-thrust farts and what to do about smegma, keep in mind that you will have to give something back conversationally in order to justify your admittance to the fold. Alas this will likely involve more exposure to disco and West End musicals than could possibly be good for your sanity. Just keep telling yourself that like with alcohol, you will eventually develop a modicum of tolerance, if not a connoisseurship.

N.B. Any man who tries to impress you using the same technique is: gay, and quite possibly short-sighted.

CHAPTER 10

A Man's POV

— top tips from the horse's mouth

Bottom line, however, is that no matter how much care and attention you give to observing Men in their natural habitat, no one knows the male mind better than a man himself.

I know, it flies directly in the face of all received wisdom. We women are meant to be the introspective sex, not them beastly boys. But when coaxed out of their masculine shells, I think you'll find men can be eloquent, thoughtful, and more to the point, spot-on about their observations of what it is that actually makes others of their kind tick. Go figure.

Don't be That Girl

If you've ever wondered what exactly turned your dating situation, budding relationship, or full-on lurve from red-hot to ice-cold in a matter of minutes, chances are, it was something the man saw as a serious red flag but that you were simply unaware of.

So in the pursuit of scientific excellence I dug deep –
in other words, bribed men with beer and/or sex – and
popped the question: just what sort of girl is it that you
would never, ever date again? The kind who could
inspire you to invent, build, and travel in a time
machine, simply for the explicit purpose of warning
your younger self against?

These were the top responses...

1. All the Gear and No Idea

Apparently there is a variety of woman – not altogether
rare from what I understand – that has taken on the
'men like visual stimuli' portion of sexual knowledge,
but not the 'but they don't like a tease' bit. In other
words, a woman whose bedroom is kitted out all
harem-style, who owns enough frillies to put Agent
Provocateur to shame, but when it gets down to the
business does not have it dirty. At all. No suck, just
fuck. In missionary. And you come inside or not at all.

'Oh yeah, I remember her,' N says. 'Lacy, silver lin-
gerie, stiletto heels, always – always – wore real
stockings with garters, and you could see them through
her tight skirts. She just looked like sex on legs and
knew it. But once you got her into bed it was strict missionary, don't touch the hair, don't come on her face,
just inside... boring.'

Now every woman has her preferences, and while
some of them may seem strange or even arbitrary, we
are permitted that from time to time. Some girls like
rough anal, but can't bear the thought of come on their

174

faces. Fair play. And for some women, a straight-up vaginal banging is exactly what gets them off. True, those women are as rare as a unicorn's pubes, but they do exist.

However, personal preference is no excuse, none whatsoever, to deny a man any sort of the variety he craves. If all you want is the feeling of being desired and serviced, but are prepared to give very little back in the way of action, that is the worst sort of tease. And someone who looks the part of adventurous temptress, but flat-out refuses to make good on that promise, will certainly get her straight vaginal banging. And then no phone call the next day. Or indeed ever again.

'It was like she'd looked at the beginning parts of porn and decided that is what gets men off, not the actual sex act,' he grumbled. 'All the gear and no idea.'

2. Clingy McStatic of the Hertfordshire Clingons

Actual messages left on a friend's answerphone. Yes, he saved them. Yes, he plays them for everyone to laugh at. Yes, this is exactly why any message you ever leave a man should be of the 'it's me, I rang, ring me back' variety, and only one of those at the most.

Actual names have been changed.

'Hey, Matthew, it's Sara. It was so nice to meet you last night. I really enjoyed talking to you after everything I've been through recently. You're a really good listener and I felt so much better for being able to get everything off my chest. And, look, I'm sorry if you got the wrong idea when I came back to yours. I'm not usually that kind of girl, it takes someone special for me to be able to... get close, to open up, you know, because of the way I've been hurt. But something about you seemed so right and I don't regret it at all. Give me a call when you get this message. Bye. It's Sara, by the way, from last night. Bye.'

'Hey Matthew, it's Sara. Sorry about the rambling message, I guess I feel like I can really open up to you. Anyway, I'm in the mood for cooking tonight and you said that you like Italian. Or was it Thai? Well, anyway, why don't you come round after work and I'll cook you a nice meal. My parents will be in, but I'm sure they'll really like you. Don't worry, you can sleep over, they're cool. You can come round at 7.30. Don't be late! Bye. Give me a call when you get this message. Bye.'

'Hey Matthew, it's Sara. Hi, I was just wondering how you spell your name. I've got it in my phone with two Ts but then I remembered this guy came into work once, and I spelt his name with two Ts, and he was all like, "actually, it's one T" so I thought I'd ask. One T? I mean, that's stupid, I mean, isn't that spelling it wrong? If you spell yours with one T, then I'm really sorry. I'm always fucking up like this. Anyway, I'd better go, but give me a call when you get this message. Lots of love — sorry, I mean, see you later. Bye.'

'Hi Matthew, look, I hope you didn't get the wrong end of the stick earlier when I said, well it might have sounded like I said something that I didn't actually say, I don't want you to think I'm some nutter. I mean, my friends say I'm mad, but, you know, not in a bad way. Anyway, give me a call because mum said she'd get the shopping for tonight I just wanted to double check whether you wanted Thai or Italian, or was it Chinese? Anyway, she's leaving in ten minutes, so give me a call. Bye.'

'Matthew? It's Sara. I don't know why you didn't return any of my messages yesterday. I think that's rude and immature and don't bother telling me your battery's died because I have delivery reports on my mobile and I got one for the text I sent you yesterday so I know your phone's on. If you don't want to talk to me then you could at least say it to my face, because that's what adults do. My mother went out to get the shopping and I waited all night, dinner was ruined by the way, don't bother calling. I hope you're happy. Goodbye.'

'Matthew, it's over. I never want to see or speak to you again. I can't believe how wrong I was about you. I can't believe I opened up to you, let you get close. You're just like all the rest, you pretend you care but you don't. Are you happy now? Kicking a girl when she's down? Well, I'm too good for you, I deserve better than this. I don't ever want to speak to you again. Goodbye. It's Sara, by the way.'

3. The Shameless Hussy

I have often been accused of favouring men to the point of being misogynist.

It may be true. And if so, there are reasons. You must admit, for all the ways in which men can and do act terribly in relationships, they are absolutely nothing compared to the damage a similarly deviously inclined woman can do. Because he is far too much of a gentleman and would never tell the story himself, I am going to tell this on behalf of my ex, and now best mate, A4.

In the first week of his first year of university, A4 met Alex. Alex was sweet, smart, and lived in the same hall of residence. And like A4, she had been raised Catholic.

They went out with friends a few times, got on very well, and to no one's surprise were shortly a couple. However, Alex was dedicated to her religion, and specified that while she desired A4 sexually, she wanted to save full intercourse for marriage. A4, being a sweet bloke, and somewhat inclined in that direction himself, agreed. She was, after all, worth waiting for. After the second year, they moved in together.

Fast-forward four years. A4 was in postgraduate studies; Alex was in professional training. They were still living together. And that is when the bombshell drops:

Alex had fallen in love with someone else.

And was having sex with him.

For fuck's sake. There really is no excuse in this, or indeed any other rational universe, for people to behave in such a manner. In fact when I am elected Queen for Life of the Universe, such people will be put to death.

They lived together. Slept in the same bed for years. And never once had sex. While she was fucking someone else.

So informed, I was happy to relieve A4 of his virginity, and so started the glorious friendship we enjoy to this day. But if ever I have the misfortune to run across that woman – or indeed if it is her bad fortune to run into me – I would swing for her. Truly.

4. The Over-Sharer

My friend N went out with a woman he had been fancying for some time. She was well-put together, elegant, and importantly in his mind, probably up for very dirty sex. (Then again he tends to make that assumption about everyone unless informed otherwise.)

N asked the lass out once every few weeks for several months before she relented – a recent breakup dissuading her from dipping a toe back in the waters of single life, apparently. When she finally gave in – and *she* asked *him* – he was overjoyed.

For their first date he took her to a Chinese restaurant. They were getting on well and the food was lovely. Just as he was about to pop into his mouth a battered piece of chicken glistening with sweet and sour sauce she said, 'That looks just like my miscarriage did'.

Suffice it to say, there was not a second date. He did shag her though.

Then there was the woman who, in bed for the first time with A1, said: 'My ex-boyfriend had the biggest cock I've ever seen.' Right. Before. Entry.

5. The Mountain-into-Molehill Architect

'So what's the most irritating thing women do in relationships?' I asked.

The MIF (Man I'm Fucking) looked over from the kitchen, where he was making coffee, and raised an eyebrow. 'Crap post-sex questions like this,' he said.

'No, seriously, it's for a book. What's the most irritating thing women consistently do, that you wish they wouldn't?'

He went quiet and thoughtful. *Ah shite*, I thought, *he's thinking of something I did.* 'Well I hope you don't take offence at this...'

'No, it's okay, it's for science.' Social science anyway.

'That nonsense you pulled last night was irritating.'

I nodded. I'd even known at the time. We were meant to be meeting his friends, only they didn't have their plans set. I was already bored and dying to go out, so when he said they were *probably* meeting at a particular place, I immediately headed out to meet them there. Three quarters of an hour later, and having dragged myself halfway across town, I received a text – it wasn't to be that pub after all, but another one not five minutes from my house. Annoyed by the change, and the inevitable taxi ride it would take in order to meet them at all, I text the MIF: *Fine. Catch you another time.*

He phoned instantly. 'What do you mean, catch me another time? I want to see you.'

'But I've come all the way here,' I said. 'It's going to be expensive to get back.'

'Hey, I didn't say we were definitely going there,' he said. 'I said they said they were possibly going there.' I heard the edge in his voice rising, a touch of anger.

'You're the one who wanted to go out early.'

'Okay, okay,' I said, though feeling somewhat less than conciliatory. 'It's not a big deal. I'm here now so I'll stay a bit and join you later.'

I was huffy. Out of pride I stayed at the first place and had a drink (alone), then thought better of it, caught a taxi and met the MIF and his friends.

'Sorry,' I said from the sofa, watching him depress the plunger on the cafetiere. 'In my defence it was the first day of my period.'

'Yeah, the thought had occurred to me,' he said.

'What do you feel when someone does that?'

He shrugged and poured two mugs of steaming Kenyan. 'If it's someone you know a bit and like, you write a certain amount of it off,' he said. 'You give them the benefit of the doubt because if most of the time things go smoothly, then it's no big deal. But if it happens too often or too early then you decide she probably isn't worth the effort because it will only get worse over time, and lose her number.'

There you have it. Take-away lesson here? Some things are worth fighting about. Most things aren't. Changed plans in which one pub is exchanged for another, and he definitely wants to see you, certainly aren't. Don't be the girl who is so attached to winning every single point that in the end the man decides you're not worth it. Also 'tis better to be fashionably late and end up in the right place than to be stuck halfway across town waiting on a taxi.

6. The Disappearing Blowjob

So later that night, MIF and I were in bed. 'You know what else I hate?'

I rolled my eyes. Luckily, the lights were out and he couldn't see. But it's a classic – plant an idea in a man's mind and he will chew it over endlessly. 'Is this another one about me?'

'Uh? No. It's just that I hate it when you start officially dating someone, and you never get oral sex again.'

'You know what they say about marriage,' I said. 'It's where blowjobs go to die.'

He was quiet a few minutes. Good, I thought. Now I can get some sleep. 'You know what else is irritating?'

Ugh, who cares? I have enough for the book now. Who ever heard of a Top Six list? 'No, what?'

'When a woman just lies there. Expects you to do all the work. And demands a lot of it.'

'In general?'

'No, in bed. There was a girl I got with three, maybe four times. By the last time I was like, I'm hanging out here, and she's not doing anything.'

If there's anything that makes for ~~great~~ rubbish pillow talk, it's men talking about what they hate in ex-lovers. However, that's their problem, and for another book. 'A cumbucket basically.'

'Yeah. I didn't call her back after that.'

'Great. Thanks for the input. Good night.'

Get the Sex You Want: alpha male tactics for women

It is a truth universally acknowledged that a one-night stand will never lead to a relationship.

Or is it? According to N, 'almost all of my long-term relationships have started as one-night stands that just carried on and on.' And as someone currently dating a person she met in the Casual Relationships small ads, well... what seems like a universal truth for women is somewhat less universal, it would seem, to the men.

However, you can never assume that a one-nighter will lead to something more. In fact, as with the start of all relationships, it's probably best you don't.

Some of my male friends do indeed conform to the easy-equals-not-girlfriend-material view of women. But what they all agreed on was that there should be a set of ground rules for one-nighters: a code of conduct, if you will. I'm going to leave the subject of the man's responsibility for now... and address the women.

So after consulting several men, I've managed to compile a list of one-off sex Dos and Don'ts that, with luck, will not only give you a satisfying sex experience (or at least, as much of one as random never-to-be-repeated lust can offer, which is potentially great but often disappointing) but also preserve your dignity.

How to (and how not to) have a one-night stand

1. *Choose when still sober.* While the temptation to dive at the closest male individual as soon as the opening strains of 'I've Had the Time of My Life' come on, by then your powers of discernment will well and truly be shot. I highly recommend buying no fresh drinks after midnight.

   Take mental notes early, identify targets, and be willing to go home alone: 9 a.m. Sunday is no time to discover you ended up in bed with Jimmy Saville.

2. *Have your own protection.* One or two condoms tucked in a bag or discreetly in a bedside drawer is a very, very good idea. A significant sample of my male friends are either crap at pre-planning or condom-shy... I leave it to you to decide which.

   That said, no need to show off the Tesco Value 500-pack of prophylactics straight away. Particularly if it's half-empty.

3. *Your place, your pickup... your pleasure.* Always keep in mind that you did the choosing, so remember it is about your enjoyment of the experience, not his.

   In other words, don't let him be a three-pump chump. Men like a woman who participates, not a girl who just lies back and thinks of Swindon. If nothing else, do everything in your power to make the sex part enjoyable.

4. *Remove makeup before going to sleep.* No one wants to wake up next to a half-melted horror, and if you're

the sort of girl apt to look in the mirror with regrets the morning after, panda eyes won't improve that feeling.

The one person who objected to this was N, but then, he likes to see evidence of having done it rough and dirty. Otherwise, ladies, baby wipes are your friend.

5. *For the love of god, don't cook.* One women's magazine (that shall remain nameless) advised women to whip up a full English the morning after – making you, apparently, a 'goddess' to him.

Goddess? Mum, more like. If you come over all domestic, coffee is just about acceptable. Anything more screams desperation.

6. *Don't go all clingy on him next morning and force him into an awkward shopping trip/greasy spoon/walk in the park.* One, it's ever so tacky; two, while one-nighters may only rarely turn into relationships, one-nighters followed by fake coupledom never do.

Kick him out quickly, run yourself a hot bath, and smile – this is your prerogative as a single woman.

Men on love, and what they love

Men love to be in love.

Yes, you read that right. Men. Love. To be in love.

Honestly. Who was Saint Valentine? A man. Designers of the world's most beautiful clothes? Men. Dude what directed that *Four Weddings* and *Love, Actually* shite? Man. Shakespeare's sonnets? Maybe not written by *that* man, but almost certainly by *a* man.

They may not show it in the same way – and they may arguably be better at discerning mere lust from real love, though the jury is still out – but there is no denying that they all want to find someone and fall hard.

So what makes a woman the sort of person a man will fall in love with? Her clothes? Her hair? Her CV?

All mere details, and not even relevant ones, apparently.

When I asked men what were the main things that made them fall for a woman, you can bet I got answers all over the spectrum from baking amazing peanut butter cookies (my current man's ex, which little does he know means I will *never* do that) from waking him up with a blowjob (N, of course).

But while the areas of disagreement varied wildly, there was a core of agreement on qualities that make a man fall in love. No, we're not talking attraction here – any damn'd fule can make a man salivate with the right dress and the right lighting. But what qualities in a woman make him start thinking about commitment? Here were the big three...

1. A woman who is passionate

Not just in the bedroom. When a man says he's attracted to a woman with passion, he means the non-relationship variety. She could be crazy about her work, her hobbies, the place she lives, anything, as long as she shows distinct interest in things that are not him.

This goes double if you are considering compromising your packed schedule just to spend more time with a man. Trust me, if he's keen, he will find a way around your to-ings and fro-ings. Example: I go running after work on Tuesdays and then out for a beer with the girls; if my man wants to see me, he can come into town after and buy me a meal, and that's that. I'm not going to hightail it home to shower, shave and whip up a four-course masterpiece just because he requires attention. And what do you know, if he has to work for a slice of my time, he appreciates it more. He asks more questions about my day, how the running went, how my friends are doing. He loves to pick up the bill. Men are just sort of funny like that.

N points out that most of his girlfriends, both long- and short-term, have been somehow involved in sport. The dedication to making something work, the ability to love something even when it's not going well... those are qualities that signal to man that he is dealing with someone worth fighting for.

2. A woman who understands space

This really can't be emphasised enough. Men have their own passions and interests too, and you should respect them. They have their own friends, their own history, and while it's great to be at the point in a relationship where you are finishing each other's stories and sharing new experiences together, sometimes he will need to reconnect with the single version of himself.

My guy, for instance, has a Wednesday-night appointment that is sacrosanct. It is the evening he goes to meet the guys, many of whom I've only met in passing. Sometimes they play football; sometimes they go to the gym or for a beer. And when he comes home – often well past my bedtime – I don't ask what went down. It's guy time. It's his.

Respect his privacy and his right to a private life. Unless your man is a proven cheater on you – in which case, why the fuck are you still hanging around, lady? – there is no reason to make him feel Guilty Until Proven Innocent. And from watching the relationships of those around me, I can see how an edge of mistrust can push a man to act up more. If he reckons he's already bollocks-deep in shit, then he figures he might as well go all the way.

Think of it this way – if you want him to respect your family and friendships, you have to respect his. One major way to signal respect to a man is not to meddle. Show him trust and he will trust you in return.

3. A woman who is confident

Confidence is not only the number one attractor – this was universal – it is also the number one quality in a 'keeper'. 'I love a woman who I know could have someone else at any time, but stays with me,' says P. 'I get a thrill when I notice other men looking at her.'

If you want to be the girl who bags a 10, *be* a 10. Sound unlikely, or at least genetically improbable? Think again. *Passing* for good-looking is not the same as *being* good-looking. Any fool can be born with a genetic advantage, but it takes real talent to leave the impression of grace and beauty through her personality.

Smile, and you go up a point or two. Be someone who is so switched-on, interesting, and fun to be around that men will think you're gorgeous.

I tell you this from experience, as someone who is a solid 7, maybe an 8 in photos: looks matter, but only a bit. Personality really does influence how physically attractive other people will think you are. Have swagger. After getting the man, don't lose it.

And how do you preserve your swagger? Through flirting, of course. There seems to be an unwritten rule that flirting stops once a committed relationship is achieved — and that is precisely the wrong thing to do. Smiling and friendly chat, with an edge of swagger, keeps things fresh. Flirt subtly with the men you meet — this is including, and especially, your man — and his estimation of you will go up and up.

Remember, you're the prize. You are the one who chose him, and you are the one who continues to do so. You don't settle, and he needs to know about it. He needs to see you being dynamic and desired, and to want to live up to that.

In fact, you can generalise all three rules to just this one. Why? Because if you are passionate about something, that raises your confidence through competence and involvement. And if you are confident, it means you are less threatened by a man having his own interests and needs separate from you and your relationship with him.

CHAPTER 11

To Sum Up

— in conclusion, one last thing, and epilogue

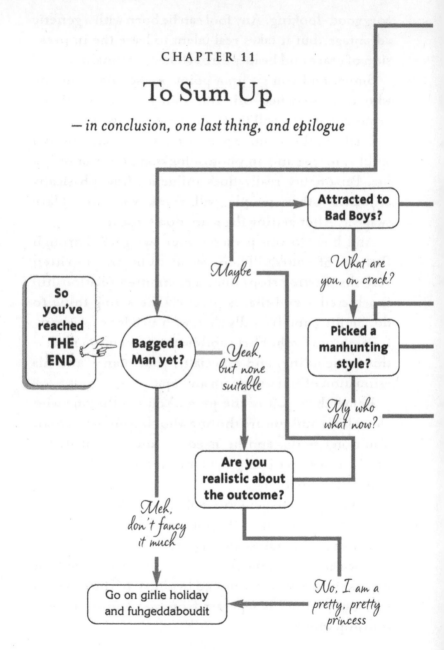

So you've reached **THE END**

Bagged a Man yet?

Maybe

Attracted to Bad Boys?

What are you, on crack?

Picked a manhunting style?

My who what now?

Yeah, but none suitable

Are you realistic about the outcome?

Meh, don't fancy it much

Go on girlie holiday and fuhgeddaboudit

No, I am a pretty, pretty princess

I can't help it! They're so hot!! →

Back up two (or more) chapters and we'll talk later

No, wondering why I still pick jerks →

Hey, What can I do? I'm not perfect. Far from it. All I got is my own limited experience to go on here. And let's be honest, I'm just a hooker, you know? If I had the magic bullets as re: men, I probably would have spent my twenties in a series of loving, fulfilling relationships instead of hooking up with random guys for cash and having my heart broken by a series of idiots. Think of it this way: at least hopefully you learned something from my mistakes instead of living the horror yourself

Hoping for a different result?

Yes! You got me completely wrong! →

Yeah but no but . . . →

Yes →

Yeah. You're mean →

'Sigh' start again at Chapter 1. You'll be fine

Soz, babes. No one gets it right all the time

Whoah, hold up. I didn't know you were so sensitive about it

Then get out there and put it into practice, lady. I can't hold your hand the entire way

Water under the bridge. We still cool?

Cool ← *Um, I guess so*

Index

Notes

Notes

Notes

Notes

Notes